THE WORLD'S GREATEST
ALIEN ABDUCTIONS

ACKNOWLEDGEMENTS

Corbis UK Ltd 130
Corbis-Bettmann 19, 22, 32, 40, 59, 70, 77, 85, 94, 103, 112, 121
Hulton Getty Picture Collection 166
Hulton Deutsch/Bettmann 175
Rex Features 184
Tony Stone Images 49, 139, 150, 157

THE WORLD'S GREATEST
ALIEN ABDUCTIONS

Nigel Cawthorne

CHANCELLOR
PRESS

This edition first published in 1999 by Chancellor Press,
an imprint of Bounty Books,
a division of Octopus Publishing Group Ltd,
2-4 Heron Quays, London E14 4JP

Reprinted 2000

ISBN 0 75370 087 5

Printed and bound in Great Britain by
Mackays of Chatham plc, Chatham, Kent

Contents

Introduction

It is incredible: first they came to buzz us, then they came to talk to us and now aliens are coming to Earth to abduct us. And it is getting worse.

Since the term 'flying saucer' was first coined in 1947, a staggering 40 million unidentified flying object (UFO) sightings have been logged. One in ten Americans claims to have had some sort of encounter with an alien. Over 30 UFO crash landings have been reported and abduction reports run into the tens of thousands.

Now many of these people could be deluded . . . or, indeed, lying, but many of them truly believe that they are telling the truth. While some abductees have made a fortune from books and films about their experiences, others have shied away from publicity, not wanting people to think that they were cranks or just plain crazy. Some abductees have been policemen and ministers of the cloth, whose reputation and livelihoods were at stake, but they still spoke out.

True, few people have a clear recollection of being abducted; most claim that they discovered that they had been abducted when they realised that they were 'missing time'. This phenomenon occurs when an abductee has seen a UFO and then finds that they have no memory of the following period. UFO investigators use a technique called regressive hypnosis to try to uncover what happened during that missing time, in which the hypnotist puts the abductee into a trance and takes them back to relive their experiences. Sometimes the victim is so terrified by what happened that they blank it from their minds, even when they are in the deepest trance, Others recall 'false memories', which were either implanted by the aliens to cover their tracks or were evoked by the abductee to hide the awful truth from themselves. But by delicate probing the hypnotist can often reveal the details of the abduction ordeal.

Some victims are abducted just once, others many times throughout their lives. Some are constantly plagued by aliens invading their homes at night. Whole families can be abducted separately, or together.

There are several types of aliens involved. In the USA, most aliens these days are short – usually about 4 foot 6 inches (1.37m) – and look like a foetus. They have no hair, vestigial eyes and ears and huge, black, pupil-less eyes. They also have long, thin arms and three or four tapering fingers, like the eponymous ET's (extraterrestrial's). They are ugly and rarely have genitals. These forms of alien are known as 'greys', because of their grey skins.

Americans used to see aliens that were of the 'Nordic' type. They are tall and good-looking, with blond hair and blue eyes – the type that is common in Europe nowadays; however, greys seem to have been creeping into Britain recently. Nordics nearly always wear the Bacofoil suits that were so popular in 1950s' sci-fi movies. They sometimes appear with greys, but more often use small robots to carry out menial tasks for them. In South America, aliens come in a bizarre range of types. Many are hairy.

It is difficult to explain why differing types of alien should visit different continents, although some abductees say that they have been told that there is competition between the various species of alien. Experts explain that aliens are so beyond our comprehension that they manifest themselves in the various ways that different cultures have learned to understand. That is why, as human culture becomes more globalised, abductees' descriptions have become more consistent, the pundits say.

Alien abductions occur in different ways, too. Some people are lured – perhaps subliminally – to deserted spots from which they can be snatched. They may then be marched up a ramp or a ladder on to the aliens' spacecraft. Sometimes the aliens come to an abductee's bedside, even while their partner is sleeping beside them, before paralysing their victim and floating them out of the bedroom window. On other occasions a car, along with all of its passengers, is beamed on board by a column of light.

Once aboard, abductees go through a range of experiences. Some are taken to distant planets, while some are given a whistle-stop tour of the Earth by creatures who say that they live on the planet but don't get out much. Others are shown films depicting the destruction of the Earth, or another planet, and are warned of the dangers of war and pollution. Yet others are seized for medical experimentation or sexual purposes.

Strangely enough, most of the good-looking, female aliens head for

South America, from which they abduct Latin lovers for a night of passion on their spacecraft. In North America and Britain it is the male aliens who grab human women and then seduce or rape them. The aliens often complain that their race cannot reproduce and explain that they are trying to create hybrid babies with earthlings. As a result, lots of female abductees say that they have been put through unpleasant gynaecological examinations. This is the commonest element in the abduction stories told by female abductees, who sometimes believe that their eggs have been taken. And such women also often report having implants inserted up their noses or into incisions made in their legs.

Some women find that they have been impregnated by aliens, but then mysteriously lose the baby, often after a second abduction. (It is thought that the aliens take the developing foetus and incubate it elsewhere.) Women sometimes report seeing what they believe is their hybrid offspring during later abductions.

Aliens are interested in the male genitalia, too: men recall having been fitted with suction devices and then having had their semen extracted. This, apparently, is all part of the aliens' hideous genetic experiment.

You may find some of the stories in this book. Others may sound like sexual fantasies – or sexual anxieties – that have been projected into outer space. Even so, they still represent the world's greatest alien-abduction stories. Some are hard to shake off. You may be able to identify which ones are drug-induced, or half-remembered dreams, delusions, the result of lack of sleep or motorway hypnosis, or those which are plain rubbish – it is difficult to say where the line should be drawn. But many of the stories presented here have a bizarre consistency that is not easily explained away; something is happening out there. So once you have discarded the stories that you find too incredible to be true, what you have left will undoubtedly constitute the world's greatest alien abductions.

1 ❖ The first abductions

In earlier times, people really thought that they saw angels and were abducted by fairies. Today, in our scientific age, few of us believe in angels, fairies, hobgoblins, elves or any of the other supernatural beings of medieval times. Instead, however, we see UFOs and are abducted by aliens.

An interrupted journey

Barney and Betty Hill were the archetypal Mr and Mrs America. They lived in the small town of Portsmouth, New Hampshire; Barney worked for the US Post Office, while Betty was a social worker employed by the state. Like many Americans, she believed in UFOs – her sister, Janet, had seen one four years before our story begins, in 1957. But Barney remained sceptical.

They had been up to Niagara Falls and had then driven on into Canada for a short holiday. But on the night of 19 September 1961 they heard that a hurricane was storming up the eastern seaboard; it was due to hit New Hampshire the following day. Rather than face the journey back through the chaos that the hurricane would leave its wake, they abandoned their plans to stay overnight in Montreal and turned for home.

They crossed the US border a little before 10pm, near Colebrook, New Hampshire, where they stopped at a restaurant for a bite to eat. They were tempted to stay in Colebrook overnight, but once fortified they decided that they would press on down Highway 3. They pulled out of the car park at 10.05pm. It was another 170 miles (274km) to Portsmouth and Barney reckoned that they should be home by 2.30am – or 3am at the latest.

Thirty-five miles down the highway, just south of Lancaster, Betty noticed a bright light in the sky. It was to the left of, and slightly below, the full moon. Then she noticed another light, which appeared to be becoming brighter and brighter. It seemed to be moving, but Betty could not be sure that that was not due to the movement of the car. Barney slowed down to take a look, but dismissed the light as a satellite that had gone off course.

The light stayed with them for several miles. It occasionally disappeared behind trees and hills, only to reappear again. The Hills had their dachshund, Delsey, with them, in the back of the car. The dog grew restless (animals are frequently spooked by UFO activity, the Hills learned later). They decided to pull over and let the dog out for a run. By stopping they could also observe the light while they were stationary and thus ascertain whether it was moving or not.

Always a 'worrier', as Betty put it, Barney was a little nervous about stopping: he said that he was afraid of the bears that inhabited the hills. Betty laughed at him and they then found a place to stop which had good all-round vision. On getting out of the car they saw that the light was moving all right, but they could still not make out what it was. It was certainly not a star, as at one point it moved in front of the moon. They got the dog back into the car and drove on.

Barney suggested that the lights belonged to an aircraft – a helicopter, perhaps. Whatever the airborne vehicle was, it now appeared to be following them. They stopped again a couple of times to try to identify it. It soon became clear that it was neither a satellite nor an aircraft as it seemed to hover without motion before setting off with a burst of incredible speed. At one point it appeared to be circling them.

Betty was convinced that it was UFO because it was festooned with multi-coloured lights that flashed out beams. Looking through a pair of binoculars that they kept in the car she could see what she took to be an alien spacecraft. It had a fuselage, but no wings, and whatever powered it made no noise at all.

They were now on a remote section of the road. Not even the official rangers patrolled there and people had been known to freeze to death if their cars broke down, so private car-recovery firms covered the area. They passed a motel and for a moment considered stopping, but the film *Psycho* was in everyone's minds back then and no car had passed them for miles.

As they drove past a resort area called Indian Head, curiosity finally got the better of Barney and he suddenly stopped in the middle of the road. Leaving Betty in the car, he took the binoculars and got out to take a better look at the craft, which had dropped down level with the height of the trees. Barney could see a double row of windows and approached within 50 feet (15m) of the spacecraft. Through the windows he saw around half-a-dozen beings looking at him. He thought that they were wearing shiny, silver uniforms, but what he remembered most clearly was their curious, hypnotic eyes. Betty screamed for him to return to the car, but Barney stared on, oblivious to her.

What seemed to be landing gear then appeared beneath the craft. This broke the spell and Barney turned and ran back to the car. He jumped in and set off at high speed, convinced that the aliens intended to capture them. Betty looked around, but the craft had disappeared. It was then that they heard a strange beeping sound as a tingling feeling of drowsiness came over them. Next they heard a second set of beeps, directly after the first, it seemed to them. The drowsiness left them and they found themselves 35 miles (56km) beyond Indian Head, with no recollection of having travelled there. 'Now do you believe in UFOs? Betty asked casually. Barney replied that he did not.

A signpost indicated that they were now 17 miles (27km) from Concord, New Hampshire, and their sense of disorientation left them. By the time that they reached home the sun had almost risen. They checked their watches, only to find that they had stopped, but the clock in the kitchen said that it was five o'clock. Two hours had gone 'missing'.

They had a light snack, went to bed and slept until three in the afternoon. By the time that they awoke Barney had put the whole thing out of his mind, but Betty phoned her sister and told her that she, too, had seen a UFO. Janet had a neighbour who was a physicist. He suggested that Betty check the bodywork of her car with a compass in case it had been subjected to any strong, electromagnetic field. Betty did just that and found a dozen magnetic hot spots on the boot which coincided with shiny patches on the paintwork. Barney, however, was not impressed.

Janet had another friend, who was a former chief of police. He suggested that Betty call the United States Air Force and report the sighting, so Betty called Pease Air Force Base. The officer to whom she spoke seemed interested in her description of the craft, but Betty did not describe the occupants; only Barney had seen them. Nevertheless, a report was forwarded to the staff of Project Blue Book, the official UFO study group at Wright-Patterson Air Force Base in Ohio.

Although Barney pushed the incident to the back of his mind, Betty could not. She went to the library and began reading up on UFOs. One of the books that she read was *The UFO Conspiracy* by Donald Keyhoe, a former major in the US Marine Corps. On 26 September 1961, just one week after her own sighting, she wrote to Keyhoe, who was now the director of the National Investigations Committee on Aerial Phenomena (NICAP), the leading UFO-research group of its day. Three days after writing the letter, Betty began to have a series of disturbing dreams in which she was taken aboard an alien spacecraft and subjected to a medical examination.

The NICAP took her letter seriously and sent scientific adviser Walter Webb to interview the Hills. He was impressed by them. They were pillars of the community and stalwarts of the local church. A mixed-race couple – unusual in New England during the 1960s – they were also active in the National Association for the Advancement of Colored People. Barney sat on the New Hampshire Civil Rights Commission, too. Webb was further-more struck by the way in which the couple constantly played down what they had seen.

Webb's report prompted two more NICAP investigators, Robert Hohman and C D Jackson, to visit the Hills. James MacDonald, a friend of the Hills who had recently retired from the US Air Force Intelligence, was also present at the meeting. It was MacDonald who floated the idea of using hypnosis to discover what had happened during the Hills' missing two hours. Captain Ben Swett from Pease Air Force Base also thought that this might be a good idea.

In the summer of 1962 Barney became ill. His symptoms included exhaustion, high blood pressure and stomach ulcers. His doctor thought that the cause of his problems might be psychological and sent him to see Dr Duncan Stephens, a psychiatrist. Barney found it difficult to open up to Dr Stephens on the subject of his UFO sighting, which was one possible cause of the anxiety from which he was plainly suffering. When he finally did, however, he brought up the idea of using hypnosis to find out what had really happened. Dr Stephens agreed and sent him to see Dr Benjamin Simon, a hypnotherapist in Boston.

Barney's first consultation with Dr Simon was in December 1962. Although the appointment was for Barney alone, Betty came along, too, because in view of her dreams she thought that both of them might need treatment. The hypnotic sessions began in January 1963 and continued for six months. Dr Simon used regressional techniques with which to take the Hills back to the missing two hours. He treated them separately, so that each of their accounts would not be tainted by the other's experience or perception of it. And it was only towards the end of the six months that he played any of the tapes of the sessions back to the Hills to help them to come to terms with what had happened.

The story that emerged under hypnosis was as follows. After Barney had sped away from the craft he grew calmer. Then he had inexplicably turned off the main road, down a track, seemingly heading towards a light that he thought was the setting moon. But the track was blocked by a gaggle of figures. Betty thought that they were men whose car had broken down, while Barney feared that they were about to be robbed.

One of the figures held a strange device in its hand, which it pointed it at the Hills. At that moment the engine of the Hills' car cut out. As the figures approached, Betty, realising that something was wrong, got out of the car and tried to run, but they grabbed her. It was then that she saw that they were not men at all, but small, hairless, ashen-coloured beings, with large heads, high foreheads and huge eyes. Barney just remembered that they were humanoid, but he saw little beyond the strange, slanting eyes. They had a hypnotic effect on him and slowly he closed his own.

The Hills were taken on board the alien's spacecraft, which had landed nearby. They were led to separate rooms, where they were subjected to medical examinations. Samples of blood and skin were taken from them and the aliens were particularly interested in Barney's false teeth. A suction device was also placed over his groin, which caused him considerable discomfort. (It presumably took a sperm sample.) The shape of the suction cup matched a circular wart that subsequently developed on Barney's groin.

The aliens unzipped Betty's dress and took off her clothes. They them made her undergo a gynaecological examination. A long needle was next inserted into her navel, in what they told her was a pregnancy test. They also showed her what has since come to be known as the 'Star Map', a chart delineating their trade routes and the details of their expeditions. Betty asked where their home planet was. The larger being, whom Betty took to be their leader, asked her where the Earth was on the map, but Betty could not show them. The leader then said that there was little point in telling her where they had come from because she did not know where her own planet was on the map. Betty reproduced the Star Map under hypnosis and amateur astronomer Marjorie Fish believes that she has found a match of it in space. Her interpretation of Betty's Star Map leads her to believe that the aliens were from Zeta Reticuli, a binary-star system some 37 light years from Earth.

The redoubtable Betty was eager to take something from the craft that would prove that she had had an encounter with aliens, and therefore persuaded them to give her a book. However, the leader took it back before she left the ship, having presumably decided that the Hills would not be allowed to remember the encounter. Betty in turn became upset, and swore that she would remember, whatever happened. The Hills were then dressed and taken back to their car. They watched the alien spacecraft depart before taking to the road again. Something implanted by the aliens in their subconscious minds then wiped all recollection of the experience from their memories.

Dr Simon had never heard anything like this tale and had no idea of what to do next. He believed that the Hills were telling the truth, but was terrified that if the story got out his own reputation would be ruined and hypnosis would be discredited as a psychiatric tool. His fears were not unfounded: in 1965 a series of unauthorised articles published in a Boston newspaper leaked the story, which made the Hills sound like kooks.

The Hills were also concerned that the implausible story of their abduction would tarnish their reputations if it were made public and confided their fears to Dr Simon. Together they subsequently approached the well-known local writer John G Fuller and asked him to put their side of the story in writing. He agreed, and they consequently collaborated on the book *The Interrupted Journey: Two Lost Hours Aboard a Flying Saucer*. When *Look* magazine picked up the story in 1966 the two issues that carried the Hills' tale broke all records at the news-stands. The story was syndicated world-wide and offers for the film rights came flooding in – the lowest bid was $300,000. Their tale was eventually recreated in a made-for-TV movie called *The UFO Incident*, starring James Earl Jones as Barney and Estelle Parsons as Betty.

Betty took a lie-detector test on national television, which indicated that she was telling the truth. Detailed scrutiny of the Hills' lives revealed them to be people of the highest integrity. Their story seems unshakeable, and although Barney died in 1969 30 years later Betty was still telling the same tale. So, is it true?

The UFO-sceptic Robert Sheaffer investigated the details of the Hills' abduction. Trained as he was in astronomy, he pointed out that the first light that they had seen, close to the disc of the full moon, was, in all likelihood, Saturn and that the second, brighter light was probably Jupiter. (Indeed, around 30 per cent of all supposed UFO sightings are actually of celestial bodies, which viewers frequently report appear to move, wiggle and dart about. During World War II, for example, crews of the US Air Force (USAF) B-29 bombers flying from the Mariana Islands on bombing missions over Japan reported that they were being followed by an enemy aircraft that was fitted with bright searchlights. They believed that it was picking them out for attack by Japanese fighter planes. For several weeks the B-29 gunners tried to shoot it down, only giving up when they discovered that they had been blasting away at the planet Venus. USAF planes on UFO-intercept missions have also since found themselves chasing celestial bodies.)

Another UFO-sceptic, the author Philip J Klass, interviewed Dr Simon just weeks after the Hills' story appeared in *Look* magazine. Simon said openly that he did not believe what the Hills had told him, even though he stood to make money from the sales of the book, as well as from any film deal. He said that he had also told the senior editors of *Look* magazine that he did not accept that the Hills had been abducted by aliens, although he had a financial stake in the articles that they were about to publish, too.

Dr Simon believed that it was a simple case of *folie à deux* (joint madness): both Barney and Betty Hill were absolutely convinced that the abduction had happened, but it was simply a shared delusion. Regressive hypnosis, he said, is not a magical gateway to the truth, but rather an aid to human beings' all-too-fallible memories. (Indeed, dreams, fantasies and material from books and films can easily become mixed up with memories of real events; however, statistics indicate that some 50 per cent of alien-abduction cases are 'discovered' under regressive hypnosis.)

Dr Simon furthermore said that Betty had not started dreaming about being abducted by aliens until she began reading up about UFOs in the local library. Although Barney was not interested in Betty's nightmares, she told her friends about them – often when he was within earshot, reading the paper or watching TV; he also heard her relating them to the UFO investigators who visited them. In this way he had absorbed Betty's delusion, as if by osmosis.

Dr Simon said that he had been surprised when Betty turned up at his office with her husband when Barney came for his first therapy session. The root of Barney's psychological problems, Dr Simon believed, was his guilt about leaving his first wife and their children – who were black – for Betty, a white woman. And it was Betty who had forced the subject of UFOs onto the agenda.

Reviewing the tapes of the Hills' sessions under hypnosis, Dr Simon pointed out that most of the details of their trip back from Montreal tallied with each other's version, which is what would be expected in a shared experience. But this mutual agreement was not true of the abduction: for example, Betty said that the aliens had spoken to her in lightly accented English – like the aliens in Hollywood sci-fi movies – while Barney said that they had had no mouths and had communicated by means of telepathy. Even their reactions to the experience were different. Barney had been truly terrified; under hypnosis, he had screamed out for help and had had to be reassured by the psychiatrist. But Betty had been calm throughout: although she had recounted her fear that they were about to be dissected like laboratory mice her voice had betrayed no emotion.

The magnetic 'hot spots' on the Hills' car do not bear close examination either. A compass always reacts erratically around a large body of metal, such as a car. And Betty was, by her own admission, a believer in UFOs.

But what of the missing two hours? According to their account the Hills had turned off the road, possibly because they believed that a UFO was chasing them. It was late at night, they were tired and it probably took them some time to find their way back to the right road. Two hours can easily pass quickly during a rambling detour.

Nevertheless, the Hills' story became the world's most famous alleged alien-abduction case, and it opened the floodgates, leading to a deluge of other such claims.

Flights of fantasy

It seems that Betty and Barney Hill were not the first earthlings to have been abducted and that such instances may even have been occurring for centuries. The celebrated US astronomer Carl Sagan unearthed a folk tale dating from 1645. Sagan reported:

A Cornish teenager, Anne Jeffries, was found groggy and crumpled on the floor. Much later she recalled being attacked by little men, carried paralysed to a castle in the air, seduced and returned home. She called the little men faeries. The following year she was arrested for witchcraft.

There are those of the UFO lobby who even claim that the 'angels' who appeared to Joan of Arc in 1425 and told her that she would lead her countrymen against the English were aliens. (Had she not been abducted, as they claim, England might still have a Continental foothold today.) And there are passages in the Old Testament Book of Ezekiel, as well as in the Hindu Ramayana and Mahabharata, that could be interpreted as telling of alien abductions.

On 25 October 1595, a Filipino soldier, Gil Perez, was found in the main square of Mexico City. He was dressed in a uniform bearing Filipino military insignia. The night before, the terrified man said, he had been standing guard in Manila when a thick fog had enveloped him. He lost consciousness and later awoke in Mexico City – 1,000 miles (1,609km) away. He also mentioned that the governor of the Philippines had been assassinated. Perez was promptly arrested as a deserter, but months later the news arrived that the governor of the Philippines had indeed been killed. It was then confirmed that Perez had been on sentry duty in Manila on the night in question and that he had mysteriously disappeared. He was consequently released.

In the early seventeenth century an 18-year-old nun at a convent in Agreda, Spain, called Sister Mary, claimed that she had been flown to the New World, where she had converted an Indian tribe named the Jumano to Christianity. She also said that she had seen the Earth spinning below her during her trip. She wrote details of her journey in a diary, which her superiors burnt. She was warned that she was risking being charged with heresy with such talk, but she still refused to retract her story.

Then, in 1622, Pope Urban VIII and King Philip of IV of Spain received letters from Father Alonzo de Benavides, a missionary who had been sent to New Mexico. He complained that his journey had been a waste of time because the Indians had already been converted to Christianity. They said that a lady in blue had shown them rosaries and crosses and had taught them how to celebrate Mass.

When Father de Benavides returned to Europe in 1630 he heard about Sister Mary's claims and visited her in Agreda. Questioning her, he quickly discovered that the places that she said she had visited, and the people whom she had met, corresponded exactly with his own experiences in the region. She even knew details of the local customs and folklore that few outsiders were party to. But the piece of evidence that clinched the truth of her tale, according to Father de Benavides, was a chalice that he had brought back from New Mexico, which the nuns recognised as one that had been missing from the Agreda convent.

Sister Mary was lucky: others who told similar stories suffered the punishment for heresy. In 1655, for example, a businessman who had mysteriously turned up in Portugal was hauled in front of the Roman Catholic Inquisition. He claimed to have been standing outside his office in Goa, then a Portuguese territory in India, when he was suddenly whisked into the air; seconds later, he found himself in Portugal. The Inquisition damned his tale as being evidence of witchcraft and burnt him at the stake

Famous American astronomer Carl Sagan.

A very Victorian abduction

The modern versions of UFO reports began to be made in 1896 and 1897, when people across the US Midwest saw huge, flying craft, the descriptions of which revealed a marked similarity to the airships that were then being developed in Europe. An attempted alien abduction was also reported at that time. According to the *Stockton* [California] *Evening Mail* in 1897, Colonel H G Shaw had been travelling by buggy through the Californian countryside with his companion, Camille Spooner. They were outside Lodi, early in the evening of 25 November 1896, when the 'horse stopped suddenly and gave a snort of terror'. Shaw then saw three pale, thin, 7-foot-tall (2.1m) alien beings, who emitted a soft, warbling sound.

'They were without any sort of clothing', he said. 'But they were covered with a natural growth as soft as silk to the touch and their skin was like velvet. Their faces and heads were without hair, the ears were very small, and the nose had the appearance of polished ivory, while the eyes were large and lustrous. The mouth, however, was small and it seemed they were without teeth.'

When he touched them, Shaw found that they were almost weightless. He said that he thought that they weighed less than 1oz (28g). Using their small, nail-less hands and long, narrow feet, they tried to lift him, 'probably with the intention of carrying me away' to their ship, a '150-foot-long [46m] cigar-shaped craft with a single large rudder'. But they abandoned the attempted abduction because Shaw was too heavy. Then they flashed lights at their ship and made off towards it in a loping motion, touching the ground only every 15 feet (4.6m) or so. 'With a little spring, they rose to the machine, opened a door in the side and disappeared', he said.

Shaw maintained that the aliens were from Mars and that they had been 'sent to earth for the purpose of securing one of its inhabitants'. (Presumably they later found someone lighter.) There was certainly an alien abduction two days afterwards, if the abductee is to be believed. John A Horen claimed to have met an alien who took him onto an 'airship'. They toured southern California and then flew to Hawaii. But Horen was a well-known practical joker and his wife claimed that he had been sleeping beside her throughout the night in question.

The missing regiment

A second wave of UFO sightings occurred in Europe between 1909 and 1913. This time there were no reports of aliens trying to abduct anyone; however, something strange did happen in Gallipoli, Turkey, in August 1915, during World War I. A British regiment was climbing a hill near Suvla Bay when members of a New Zealand regiment who were watching them saw six or seven clouds hovering near the hill. One of them slowly descended and the British regiment climbed into it. When the last man had disappeared the cloud lifted to reveal no sign of the British soldiers. After World War I was over, the British authorities asked the Turks what had happened to their soldiers. The Turks said that they had never captured an entire British regiment – and had never even fought the regiment concerned.

Early abduction attempts

In 1933 'ghost rockets' were reported to have appeared in northern Sweden. And during World War II 'foo fighters' – luminous balls of light – were seen following aircraft. But no one was 'spacenapped'.

The modern era of ufology began in June 1947, when pilot Kenneth Arnold was flying over the Cascade Mountains in USA's Washington state searching for the wreckage of a C-46 Marine transport plane which had crashed. Between Mount Rainer and Mount Adams, 5,000 feet (1,524m) above him, he saw a formation of flying objects travelling at between 1,300 and 1,700 miles (2,092 and 2,736km) an hour – faster than any plane of the day was capable of. They were about 23 miles (37km) away and their formation was spread over 5 miles (8km). Another search plane was also visible – a DC-4 – and Arnold estimated that the unidentified craft were about two-thirds of its size. They were shaped like rounded boomerangs, but Arnold told the press that they travelled 'like a saucer would if you skipped it across the water'. From then on, unidentified flying objects became known as 'flying saucers'.

A month later, the so-called 'Roswell Incident' occurred. It was reported that a flying saucer had exploded and that the wreckage had come down on ranch land belonging to William 'Mac' Brazel. The remains were collected by the US Air Force, which took them to the Roswell Army Air Force Base. In the interests of national security, Brazel was asked not to talk about the incident. What the USAF hauled away from the crash site has been a source of controversy ever since, but according to some accounts the debris included the dead bodies of aliens who looked remarkably like the creatures that the Hills later described.

Undeterred by this setback, aliens attempted an abduction towards the end of that month. On 23 July 1947 José Higgins, one of a band of men working near Bauru, Brazil, saw a large flying saucer land nearby. All of them, with the exception of the courageous Higgins, ran away. He stood his ground and was confronted by a group of seven-foot-tall (2.1m) aliens with round, bald heads and big eyes, whom he found strangely attractive. They tried to lure him aboard their ship, but he first asked them where they were from. In response, they drew a map of the solar system and indicated that they came from Uranus. Higgins summoned up all his willpower and managed to give them the slip. While he was hiding in the bushes he saw them cavorting about; when they tired of doing this they went back to their ship and flew off.

Another attempted alien abduction failed in France in 1950, when, on 20 May, a woman rushing home to make dinner at around 4pm was blinded by a brilliant light which also paralysed her. Two huge, black hands grabbed her from above and she thought that she was being carried off by a giant bird. The talon-like hands gave her an electric shock; they were cold, as if they were made of metal. The fingers around her neck stifled her screams and she was dragged off into a field. Suddenly her abductor dropped her and she heard him making off through the bushes. Stumbling back to the path, she felt a violent pain down her back, as if she had been burned, and noticed a strange, metallic taste in her mouth. In the distance she could see several houses, but before she could reach them she heard a great noise and was bent double by a 'violent windstorm'. Then she saw a bright light rising in the sky. After pushing on, she at last came upon the house of a lock-keeper. The lock-keeper and his family had observed the bright light, too, and the marks that they noticed on her face were consistent with her story.

The intended abductee had seen what she took to be a shooting star the previous night, but it had appeared to be rising in the sky rather than falling.

A willing victim

One of the first people who claimed to have been whisked off in a flying saucer said that he had gone quite willingly. His name was George Adamski. Born in Poland in 1891, he had emigrated to the United States

Pilot Kenneth Arnold, centre, who apparently saw a cluster of UFO's whilst searching for the scattered debris from a plane wreck.

with his parents at the age of two and the family had settled in New York. At the age of 22 Adamski joined the 13th Cavalry and served in the US Army until 1919. Then he moved to California, where he became interested in all things mystical, eventually styling himself 'professor of Oriental Mystical Philosophy'. His 'Royal Order of Tibet' set up a farming commune at Valley Center in 1940.

In 1953 Adamski published the book *Flying Saucers Have Landed*. In it, he claimed to have made numerous sightings of flying saucers, both in flight and on the ground. His credibility was enhanced by the fact that he claimed to work at the Mount Palomar Observatory, which then boasted the largest telescope in the world. (This was true, up to a point: Adamski worked at the hamburger concession at the observatory.)

Adamski said that he had seen flying saucers since 1946 – the year before Arnold had inadvertently coined the name. On 20 November 1952, he took two families – the Baileys and the Williamsons – UFO-spotting in the Californian desert. Leaving the others in their cars, Adamski trudged away from the road into the desert with his telescope. (It seems that aliens abhor crowds and traffic.) At around 12.30pm, when he was about a quarter of a mile (40m) from the road, he saw a figure whom he took to be a man who was out prospecting. The figure gestured to him and, thinking that he might need help, Adamski approached him. But the creature turned out to be no prospector and Adamski believed him to be an alien. He was about 5 feet 6 inches tall (1.65m), weighed around 135lbs (61kg) and Adamski judged him to be 28 years old. Furthermore, his eyes were grey-green, his hair was blond and flowing, his teeth were pearly white, his skin was tanned, his features were oriental and he was dressed in a one-piece, chocolate-brown jump suit.

They communicated using a mixture of telepathy and sign language, Adamski said. Adamski pointed at the sun and then counted off the numbers one, two and three on his fingers, indicating the three closest planets to the sun – Mercury, Venus and Earth. The alien gestured two, which Adamski took to mean that he came from Venus. (It has subsequently been proved, however, that Venus is entirely unsuited to supporting life. Even toughened space probes cannot withstand the bone-crushing atmospheric pressure and the constant downpour of concentrated sulphuric acid on the planet.)

The alien took Adamski to see his flying saucer, which was parked nearby. It was very small, but the alien explained that it was only a 'scout ship'. Adamski stumbled and nearly fell under the ship, but the alien grabbed him. Telepathically, he learnt that the electromagnetic power that supported the ship would have caused him serious injury; as it was, his arm was flung beneath the craft and he lost all feeling in it for several years afterwards.

The alien also conveyed a message to Adamski. (It was the same message that the silver-suited alien played by Michael Rennie delivered in the 1951 film *The Day the Earth Stood Still*.) The people of Earth, he said, were endangering the other inhabitants of the solar system with their nuclear-weapons' tests and they should therefore cease them.

Adamski told the creature that he was puzzled by the fact that aliens never landed in built-up areas. They were afraid that they would be torn apart by a mob, the alien explained. However, he also revealed that 'space brothers' were walking among humans unnoticed, so it was only the landing that was dangerous.

Adamski's contact with aliens continued on a regular basis. He frequently met 'space brothers' in the cafés and bars of southern California. They had problems in communicating though, because the language that they spoke sounded to Adamski like some ancient dialect of Chinese, which Adamski believed was the original human language. In his second book, *Inside the Spaceships*, Adamski revealed that he had become so friendly with the aliens that they took him on jaunts around the solar system in their spacecraft. Interplanetary travel was conducted in huge 'mother ships' that were several miles long; the small scout ships were usually stored on board the mother ships and were used by the aliens to hop around a planet once they had arrived on it. Adamski even produced an 8mm colour movie of one such mother ship that he claimed to have filmed at Silver Spring, Maryland. The film could not be authenticated, however.

During the course of his travels, Adamski said, he had been introduced to Martians, Saturians and Jovians, who were all remarkably humanoid in shape. They did not explain how they lived on Saturn and Jupiter. (These giant planets have no solid surface, being constituted of gas, and the pressure is such that it would crush a human like a juggernaut squashes a hedgehog.) Despite these omissions, Adamski lectured around the world on what he had seen.

One of the most interesting places that Adamski claimed to have visited was the far side of the moon. It was covered with forests, mountains and lakes and people lived there, he said. But in 1959 the Soviet probe Lunik III sent back pictures of the far side of the moon which showed it to be as sterile and cratered as the side that we can see. Adamski alleged that this revelation was a communist plot and that the Soviet Union had doctored the pictures in order to deceive the West. However, because the data subsequently collected by the US National Aeronautics and Space Administration's (NASA) space probes revealed that none of the places that Adamski claimed to have visited bore the slightest resemblance to his descriptions, many ufologists began to wonder whether Adamski had ever been abducted at all.

The sexy spacenapper

Adamski was actually pipped to the post in the alien-abduction stakes. The year before Adamski's *Inside the Spaceships* appeared, Truman Bethurum published *Aboard a Flying Saucer*. Bethurum said that he had been carrying out maintenance work on a highway in the Nevada desert when he met five aliens. They took him back to their massive spacecraft, which was 300 feet (91m) wide.

On board he met the captain, a female alien called Aura Rhanes, whom Bethurum described as a 'queen of women' and 'tops in shapeliness and beauty'. These aliens were much more advanced than the ones that Adamski had met. They spoke perfect English and Bethurum stayed up all night swapping interplanetary stories with Aura Rhanes. He was not as lucky as many people who have met attractive aliens, in that Aura Rhanes did not have sex with him.

Bethurum's aliens looked sufficiently human to be able to mingle with earthlings unnoticed; some time later, Bethurum saw Aura Rhanes drinking a glass of orange juice in a restaurant, but she ignored him. The aliens, Bethurum said, were from a planet called Clarion, which was free from disease, war and other human scourges. It was quite close to Earth, but lay on the other side of the moon, which meant that it was permanently hidden from human gaze. (However, human spacecraft have travelled around the other side of the moon since then and have reported no sign of Clarion.)

A New York return trip

In 1954 Daniel Fry published The *White Sands Incident*. In it, he claimed that he had taken a trip on an alien spacecraft. The incident had taken place in 1950, although he later said that it was in 1949. At the time he had been at the White Sands Proving Grounds in New Mexico, where the US military was trying out the rockets – and rocket scientists – that they had captured from the Germans in 1945.

One day Fry saw a large UFO land in an isolated area near White Sands. As he approached it he heard the cautionary words 'Better not touch the hull, pal: it's still hot'. These words emanated from an alien entity who was circling the Earth in a massive mother ship; the UFO that Fry could see was merely a freighter that was used for carrying cargo. He was invited aboard and the alien gave him a guided tour of the craft's propulsion system. His name was A-Lan, although he said that Fry could call him Alan if he liked. They got on famously and A-Lan offered to take Fry on a trip. They did not go anywhere exotic, like Mars, Jupiter, the far side of the moon or Clarion – instead Fry was treated to a trip to New York and back, which took just half an hour.

A-Lan explained that he was not an alien at all, but an earthling: he was descended from an ancient race which had abandoned Earth to roam the skies after a disastrous war between the inhabitants of the lost continents of Lemuria and Atlantis. Then A-Lan delivered his Michael Rennie speech and asked Fry to relate it to the world, which he accordingly did in *The White Sands Incident*. He then gave up his job in order to lecture on his experiences and to run a foundation, based on the wisdom of A-Lan, called Understanding.

Fry was often asked why it was that if creatures from outer space really wanted humans to mend their ways they did not land on Earth openly and then pursue their agenda with the appropriate authorities through the usual channels. Fry explained that change could only come about through the work of a number of enlightened individuals, not by means of aliens descending to Earth to solve humankind's problems.

Invasion of the abductors

Aircraft mechanic Orfeo Angelucci saw his first flying saucer in 1955, when it landed in a field near Los Angeles. As seems typical, the aliens welcomed him on board and explained the workings of their electromagnetic system to him. They also gave him the Michael Rennie lecture.

Angelucci subsequently began to seen aliens all over California, hanging out in cafés and bus stations. These highly developed aliens were apparently quite happy living among inferior humans.

They later took him to Neptune, Angelucci claimed, and revealed that

Jesus Christ had been an alien. Then Angelucci discovered that he himself had been an alien in a previous life. He shared this information in his 1955 book *Secret of the Saucers*, which also contained a chilling message for humankind: mend your ways or face oblivion in 1986 (this date coincided with the return of Halley's Comet).

Fortunately, the world must have heeded Angelucci's extraterrestrial message and have mended its ways, because 1986 passed without calamity: Halley's Comet came and went and the Earth survived unscathed.

A trip to the moon

Howard Menger had been plagued by visits from beautiful, blonde, female aliens since his childhood. In 1932 the first one turned up near his home in New Jersey and told him that aliens would always be with him. Despite his long acquaintanceship with these extraterrestrial nymphets, he had no sexual contact with them (which was, perhaps, just as well, since some of them claimed to be as much as 500 years old). Menger was, however, concerned about the effect that such a level of ageing would have on their figures and therefore bought them bras, only to be informed that they did not wear such things. (Indeed, when you think about it, if you lived in the weightless conditions of extraplanetary space, a bra would be entirely unnecessary.)

The male aliens whom Menger saw were tall, blond, good-looking, clad in one-piece jump suits and extremely old. Menger would cut their hair for them so that they could mingle with earthlings without attracting attention (this was in the pre-hippie days). These aliens had visited Earth many times before and had had a hand in many of the major developments made by ancient civilisations. Disturbingly, Menger said that they were responsible for the rise of the blood-thirsty Aztecs.

They took Menger on a trip to the moon, where the air, Menger said, was similar to Earth's. To prove that he had made the trip, he brought back some 'lunar potatoes', which were unfortunately confiscated by the federal government because it is illegal to import agricultural products into the continental United States.

In common with other aliens, Menger's friends told him how their propulsion system operated. Menger made an Earthly prototype of it, but it did not work. (It is strange that no matter how many times they explain it to humans no earthling has yet managed to reproduce the extraterrestrials' mode of transport. You would think that they could abduct a scientist or an engineer who might stand a chance of understanding it.)

Like many other abductees, Menger made money both from lecturing and his 1959 book From Outer Space to You. But he was luckier than some because his aliens taught him how to make extraterrestrial music, and Menger's Music From Another Planet is still available by mail order.

The missionaries

As well as trying to alert us to the possibilities of advanced forms of propulsion and the dangers of nuclear weapons, it seems that aliens are also concerned about our spiritual well-being. In 1954 Marion Keech reported that she had heard from beings on the planets Cerus and Clarion (from which latter planet Truman Bethurum's spacemen came). Apparently, the Son of God, formerly known as Jesus, was now living on Clarion under the alias Sanada. He had spotted a fault in the Earth's crust, so he contacted Keech and warned her that a great flood was going to wipe out Salt Lake City, Utah, on 21 December 1954. Keech and her followers gathered to await a great spaceship that was supposed take them to safety. It failed to show up, but fortunately there was no flood either.

Several cults have been formed around the idea that aliens will come to Earth to save humankind. Among them was Heaven's Gate, whose 39 members committed suicide in March 1997 believing that an alien spacecraft travelling behind the comet Hale-Bopp would then rescue their liberated spirits and take them to a heavenly haven.

The London taxi driver George King said that he was first contacted by aliens when he was alone in his west London flat. He was told that he had been chosen to be the voice of the Interplanetary Parliament. In order to prepare him for his role he was taken on several trips to Mars and Venus. On one of these extraterrestrial sojourns, he said, he had saved the world by diverting a menacing meteor. Unfortunately, some of the people to whom he revealed his mission in the back of his cab were sceptical about his claims. He therefore decided to go somewhere where they were more open-minded about such things and moved to California, where he set up the Aetheris Society. He and his followers found that by using the power of prayer alone they could charge up batteries that would relieve suffering all over the world.

While he was living in Los Angeles King revealed that he was visited regularly by enormous spaceships. Fortunately, they were fitted with a cloaking device which rendered them invisible, otherwise the sight of these huge ships hovering above the city would certainly have engendered panic. Even in their invisible state they apparently presented no hazard to aircraft.

Is God an astronaut?

George King's transfer of the centre of his operations to California was a good move: aliens seem to flock to the Golden State, especially if they have some quasi-religious message to impart.

On 30 January 1965 a UFO landed near the Californian home of Sid Padrick (maybe the aliens were looking for St Patrick, but Sid was as close as they got). He heard aliens telling him to 'fear not' – the same message that the heavenly host had vouchsafed to the shepherds when it appeared to them to announce that Jesus had been born.

In Padrick's case, the aliens invited him on board their flying saucer and gave him a guided tour. These beings were not as attractive as some that other abductees had met: they were essentially human in appearance, but had pointed noses and chins. Like other aliens, they said that they came from a planet in the solar system that was hidden from human view. It again had no crime, disease or any of the other drawbacks of life on Earth; everyone there 'lived as one'. But Padrick's extraterrestrial experience was unique in one respect: in an area of the ship known as the 'consulting room' he was asked whether he would like to 'pay his respects to the Supreme Deity'. Were they kidding? Padrick asked. Was God really on board? Apparently he was for after Padrick had knelt and prayed that night he truly felt the presence of God.

Padrick related his experience to officials of the United States Air Force at Hamilton Air Force Base. They took copious notes, which were then passed on to the Project Blue Book at Wright-Patterson Air Force Base. One question that the USAF was particularly interested in was how a huge spacecraft could escape radar detection. Padrick told them that the aliens' craft had a hull which absorbed energy. Energy-absorbing paint is now used on the USAF's Stealth bombers, so maybe Padrick's contact with aliens has been of some benefit to humankind. However, although some abductees do still find themselves meeting godly aliens, by 1965, the year in which Padrick met his maker aboard a flying saucer, some aliens had begun to turn decidedly kinky.

2 ✦ Sexual encounters of the alien kind

Judging by the sighting reports, thousands of aliens are visiting Earth. But what have they come for? Are they here to study humankind? Are they here to help us? Some abductees believe that they have simply come for a good time.

Looking for a Latin lover

In 1957, four years before the Hills' 'close encounter of the fourth kind', a Brazilian man named Antônio Villas-Boas had what can only be described as a 'close encounter of the fifth kind'.

Close encounters of the first kind are simple UFO sightings. Close encounters of the second kind are sightings of UFOs accompanied by the physical evidence of an alien craft – such as the grass having been pressed down where it landed, broken twigs or scorch marks having appeared on the ground or injuries having been inflicted on animals or humans. Close encounters of the third kind are those in which the human observer has contact with intelligent beings from spacecraft, while close encounters of the fourth kind are alien abductions. And close encounters of the fifth kind involve contact of a more intimate character – at least that is what Villas-Boas said had happened to him.

The 23-year-old law student had experienced close encounters of the first kind twice before. The first was on 5 October 1957, when Villas-Boas and his brother saw a bright light shining down outside the bedroom window of their home near São Francisco de Sales in central Brazil. Villas-Boas worked on the family farm in order to pay his way through law school. The second sighting took place nine days after the first, when he was out ploughing on the night of 14 October. He again saw a bright light, which appeared to be hovering over the field 150 feet (46m) above him. This time he chased the light in his tractor. The light darted around so much, however, that Villas-Boas eventually gave up his pursuit. The light then broke up into multiple beams before disappearing completely. Again, his brother had also witnessed the phenomenon.

On the next night Villas-Boas was out ploughing again when he saw a red light coming straight towards him. This time he was alone. The light came so close that he could see that it was attached to an egg-shaped craft which had three 30-foot-long (9m) legs. When it landed Villas-Boas was seized with fear. He tried to drive away, but the tractor stalled and its lights and motor died. Four aliens then clambered out of the spacecraft. They grabbed him, dragged him to the spacecraft's ladder and forced him to climb aboard. The aliens were about 5 feet (1.5m) tall, with disproportionately large heads. (As the epidemic of alien abductions increased, this became the typical description of the extraterrestrial perpetrators of encounters of the fourth and fifth kinds.)

On board the alien spacecraft, Villas-Boas was forcibly stripped. His body was anointed in a strange, colourless and odourless, viscous liquid. The aliens wore grey overalls, gloves with five fingers and helmets and talked in a strange language which he could not understand. In another room, two other aliens cut his skin and took a sample of his blood. They then left him alone and naked for about half an hour in a small, round room. Gas was pumped into it; it smelt foul and Villas-Boas vomited. He recovered, however, when a naked female alien came in. She was humanoid, around 4 feet 6 inches (1.35m) tall, with fair skin and high cheekbones; her eyes, though blue, were oriental in shape. Her face was wide, with a pointed chin. Her hair was blonde – evidently bleached blonde, because the hair in her armpits, as well as her pubic hair, was bright red. Despite her strange appearance Villas-Boas became sexually aroused. He said

> She had the most beautiful body that I have ever seen on a woman: high, shapely breasts and a narrow waist. She had broad hips, long thighs, small feet, thin hands and normal fingernails. She was much smaller than I am, and the top of her head only reached my shoulder. Alone with this woman, who made it clear to me what she wanted, I got very excited . . . I forgot everything, grabbed her and responded to her caresses. It was a normal act and she behaved like any other woman.

They had sexual intercourse twice. Satisfactory though the experience was, however, Villas-Boas said that he would have preferred a human women because he would rather have made love to a woman to whom he could talk. She did not know how to kiss either, but he imagined that her playful bites on his chin amounted to the same thing (maybe she was just avoiding his vomit-tainted breath).

Pieces of a weather balloon are identified near Roswell, New Mexico. The area is famous as the site of a supposed UFO spacecraft crash.

Despite having had sex, she then took another sperm sample from Villas-Boas and stored it in a test tube. Before she left, she rubbed her stomach and pointed upwards. Villas-Boas interpreted this to mean that she was going to have his baby, which would be raised somewhere in the skies. The disgruntled Villas-Boas later whimpered

That was what they wanted of me: a good stud to improve their stock. In the final analysis, that was all it was. I was angry, but then I decided not to worry about it. After all, I had enjoyed some pleasurable moments, even though some of the grunts that I heard coming from the alien woman's mouth at certain moments nearly spoilt everything, giving me the disagreeable impression that I was having sex with an animal.

Once his moment of post-coital contentment had passed, Villas-Boas realised that no one would believe his story without some sort of proof. He therefore tried to steal a small device from the craft, but because he had nowhere in which to conceal it he was apprehended. Nevertheless, once he was dressed again, the aliens gave him a quick tour of the craft. Like other extraterrestrials, they proudly showed off their propulsion system, which was housed in a central dome and gave off a strange, green light. Then they took him to the ladder and made it plain that he was free to go. After Villas-Boas' feet were placed safely back on the ground the spacecraft then rose slowly into the air before taking off at a dizzying speed. The whole abduction had lasted for little more than four hours.

During the days following his abduction Villas-Boas suffered from nausea and headaches. He felt an unpleasant, burning sensation around his eyes and could not sleep at night. Strange wounds developed on his arms and legs, which healed to leave scarring. The scars were the only tangible proof of his story, but he showed them to no one. Villas-Boas was also reluctant to tell anyone about his abduction, confiding only in his mother.

In 1958 he read an article about UFO sightings in a publication called Cruzeiro. He consequently contacted a journalist, Joao Martins, who took him to Rio de Janeiro to see Dr Olavo Fontes, the Brazilian representative of the Aerial Phenomena Research Organization, a world-wide UFO group that had been formed in 1952. Dr Fontes was impressed by the symptoms of trauma that Villas-Boas exhibited. Fontes diagnosed the physical problem that he had suffered as 'radiation poisoning or exposure to radiation'. He was also impressed by Villas-Boas' willingness to undergo all sorts of tests – along with the financial loss that he thereby suffered by taking time off work for them – in the hope of finding some sort of explanation for his experiences.

In 1961 the story was picked up by Dr Walter Buhler, a Brazilian UFO expert. He interviewed Villas-Boas and submitted a detailed report of his findings to the English-language journal *Flying Saucer Review*. Despite the editors' worries that they might be dealing with the sexual fantasies of a deranged young man they eventually published the story in 1964. Years later, the appeared in print in Brazil, but it was not until 1978 that Villas-Boas made any public statement about his abduction, confirming the details of the encounter on Brazilian television. He did not give lectures on the significance of his experience, however, nor did he found a cult. He had no message or warning to convey from the aliens whom he had met, nor did he write a book about his encounter or attempt to profit from it in any way. After the investigation of his abduction was completed he qualified as a lawyer and spent the rest of his life working in the legal profession, living near Brasilia with his wife and four children.

Although he was unwilling to talk about his experiences again, Villas-Boas had seemingly cleared up one question about aliens: at least we know why some of them are here. He died in 1990, saying that 30 years earlier the US government had invited him to examine the wreckage of a crashed UFO; it is assumed by many that the wreckage came from Roswell.

Alien adultery

One night in 1981, in Birstall, West Yorkshire, Jane Murphy went to bed exhausted. A few hours later she awoke. She did not open her eyes, but she knew that something was wrong: she could not hear her husband's snoring and the feeling in the room was not right.

When she eventually opened her eyes she found herself in a field near to her mother's house; she did not know how she had got there. There was a huge, metallic UFO floating above the field and then she saw a group of humanoid figures approaching her. One of them held a cloth in its hand which it put over her nose and mouth. She feigned unconsciousness, but the aliens gave her an injection that knocked her out anyway.

She came round in a strange room, surrounded by aliens. One of them was seven feet (2.1m) tall; he looked like a male human, but his eyes were totally black. A young alien woman told her that she must bathe, so she slipped off her nightdress and got into a strange tub that seemed to match the contours of her body exactly.

There was a table in the centre of the room. All the aliens had now gone, except for the tall one, who brought his face close to hers. 'I just stared into his big, black eyes', she said, 'and I knew what was going to happen.' She is unsure of whether he raped or seduced her. She was completely mesmerised by his eyes and did not resist. In fact, he lay back on the table and she climbed on top of him. Although they embraced sexually, there was very little movement and she was not even conscious of his penis inside her. She did not think about the physical act, but nevertheless felt all the sensations of normal, human sex. 'Inside me it was all happening', she said. 'At the time, I felt it was the best sex I had ever had. It seemed so strange, lying on top of this stranger, not moving yet having sex and enjoying it.'

The only thing that repelled her was his strange, inhuman smell. She looked deep into his eyes and said 'Why me?' The answer came telepathically: 'Because we love you'. She was disappointed that his profession of love was so cold: 'There was no emotion in it at all', she said. Even so, she climaxed and said that it was the best sex that she had ever had.

Afterwards, the other aliens, including several females, examined her while her sexual partner got off the table and left the room. Then she was given a gynaecological examination with a long instrument, but felt no pain. She was later taken on a tour of the ship and saw other humans on board. She was also invited to try out some pills and was given a drink. Murphy had the impression that the aliens communicated by means of telepathy.

Suddenly she found herself back in her own bed. It was 6.30am and the alarm clock had just gone off. She would have dismissed the whole incident as having been a bad dream had she not had a strong desire to take a bath and wash the strange smell of her alien lover off her body: it was not pleasant, in fact, not human at all. When she had a bath she discovered puncture marks on her body, where, she said, the aliens had injected her. Then she felt a distinctive sensation in the pit of her stomach which she remembered experiencing when she had been pregnant in the past. When her period was late she grew frightened.

She went to the doctor, who ascertained that she was not pregnant, but had a strange, vaginal infection, which was eventually cleared up with a course of powerful antibiotics. That was by no means the end of the story, however, for within a month the aliens were back, swarming all over the house and bombarding her with questions about human reproduction. She would wake at night to find them standing by her bed. Although she had no recollection of it, she was also certain that they had carried her off again.

Soon she became plagued by a dream in which she gave birth to a blond, black-eyed, alien baby. She thought that she was going mad – indeed, she was certainly on the verge of a nervous breakdown. Her GP suspected that she had been taking LSD, and although her husband said that he did not believe that she had been abducted by aliens, her stories of having great sex with a man from outer space were putting a strain on their marriage.

In desperation, Murphy contacted the British UFO Research Association's hot line, whose members debriefed her and consequently discovered that it seemed that she had been abducted numerous times, the first occasion being when she was just 16. She may well, they believed, have given birth to an alien child which was itself then abducted.

A case of rape

According to the British UFO Research Association's investigator, Barry King, a married woman from Taunton, Somerset, was driving her car near her home one night when the engine mysteriously cut out. She got out to look under the bonnet and was then grabbed from behind.

She awoke to find herself naked, tied to table and covered with a blue blanket. Three aliens in blue tunics were examining her; they were around 5 foot 6 inches tall (1.65m), with fair skins and round, emotionless eyes. Two of the aliens left. The third gave her an injection in the thigh, which made her numb; then he raped her, coldly, without emotion and she passed out. When she awoke, she was beside her car again, which now worked perfectly.

King found her story perfectly credible; she had even told her husband.

Visiting voyeurs

Yet it seems that aliens don't just want to have sex with humans – they like to watch them making love, as well. Indeed, they seem fascinated with human reproduction. David M Jacobs, of Philadelphia's Temple University, reported that a young woman who was abducted in 1988 was forced to have sex with a man who appeared to be unconscious. Without the aid of hypnosis, she later recalled that she was made to climb upon him. She straddled the comatose man and one of the aliens who was watching her told her – telepathically – to kiss him. She did not want to do so, so she put her hand on his chest and pretended to the aliens that that was a human kiss. They seemed satisfied with her explanation and then told her to touch his penis. 'Like I was supposed to scoot down below, you know', she said. 'Down low on the table.'

She said that she didn't want to have oral sex with the man and tried to persuade the aliens that earthlings did not do that. They did not force her, but their will was hard to resist. Although the man was complete immobile otherwise, he nevertheless got an erection. The aliens next wanted her to have intercourse with him. She said that she did not want to because it was immoral, but found herself doing so anyway. 'It's totally mechanical', she recounted. 'It's really bad. I don't think I have feelings or anything.'

After the man had ejaculated, the woman's mind went blank; Jacobs thinks that she was being mind-scanned at that moment. Only after that did she find herself becoming aroused (fortunately for her, the man's penis had remained erect).

'It's so weird because it's not like any normal pattern that I've ever been through', she said. All the time she had been worried that she could become pregnant by the unconscious man.

Sex with an older man

A 15-year-old girl reported having been abducted by aliens in 1959 and having been forced to have sex with an older man. She had been totally powerless. An alien had started off the assault by staring into her eyes. 'He's completely penetrating me,' she said, 'every bit of me is in my eyes. He's in my eyes . . . I can't do anything . . . He's spreading into my brain . . . totally invading me.' The invasion went on for a horribly long time. Worse still for the girl, 'He's making me feel feelings, sexual feelings . . . It must be that he's making me feel things because I don't feel them.'

Other aliens were standing around watching, and there was a human man at the end of the table who was erect. He was a big man with a bit of a paunch and was middle-aged, with receding hair. She said that the man was 'absolutely out of it'; his mouth was hanging open and his eyes were glazed over. The brainwashing alien moved aside so that she could see the older man, then he moved back again. By this time she said that her body was responding sexually, but 'I mean, I didn't know what it was at the time, what a sexual response was'. 'I knew it was very strange. It had pleasurable parts to it, but it wasn't a pleasurable situation, obviously', she said.

The man was aroused too, and the 'inevitable followed'. The aliens seem to have had the idea that she had just ovulated, and the man climbed on top of her. The alien who had initiated matters, she said, then 'zapped' her. 'All of a sudden I'm really sexually excited', she recalled. 'Overwhelmingly sexually excited.'

When the man reached the point of ejaculation the aliens pulled him off her and put a metal instrument up her vagina. She described how the aliens had then taken an egg from her before leading the man away. She claimed that this had happened to her several times.

An alien in Essex

On the night of 27 September 1985 Ted Johnson was driving down a deserted road in deepest Essex when he saw a strange light in the distance. After he had stopped and had got out of the car to see what it was he heard a low, whistling sound. The light approached so close to him that it hurt his eyes. Then there was a green flash, which knocked him to the ground and partially blinded him.

When he got to his feet he was greeted by a strangely dressed female being. Her eyes were large and her nose small; she had a slit instead of a mouth and she was glowing. In the darkness behind her Johnson spotted other luminous humanoid forms. The female alien led him to her spacecraft, where she stripped off. 'She was naked and we had sex', Johnson claimed. 'It was not different from human sex.'

So alien-human sexual encounters do not just happen in Brazil.

Spacenapped in Somerset

The 33-year-old Mrs Milan had moved from Turin, Italy, with her husband and had settled in Somerset. On 16 October 1973 the daughter of a friend asked her to drive her to her mother's house in Wellington because her mother was ill. Mrs Milan was making dinner at the time, but promised to take her later that evening.

A number of people then dropped by, so Mrs Milan finished dinner later than she had expected. Her friend's daughter had already set off to visit her mother, but Mrs Milan decided to go and see her friend anyway and left at around 10.45pm.

At around 11.15pm she found herself driving on a lonely stretch of road near Langford Budville. A yellow light then appeared in the field to her right and next her headlights dimmed and her engine cut out. After the car had coasted to a halt Mrs Milan got out and took a look at the engine. She suddenly felt a blow to her shoulder and turned around to see a metallic man, along with flashing lights. The next thing that she knew she was standing in a field looking up at a huge flying saucer, with the yellow light that she had seen from the road issuing from its windows. It was 20 feet (6m) high and 40 feet (12m) across. Grey and metallic, it stood on thick legs and emitted a humming sound. Then she blacked out again.

She awoke inside a room. She was naked and her arms and legs were strapped to a table. The metallic man stood immobile in the corner while three creatures wearing surgeons' masks and gowns performed a detailed examination of her body. They seemed to be recording their findings on a series of illuminated colour cubes along the edge of the bed. A pen-shaped probe was used to prod her. Nail parings and blood samples were taken from her body and a fair-skinned, round-eyed man passed a small scanning device over her. A suction device was fitted over her sexual organs (this was the only part of the proceedings that caused her discomfort). Throughout, she felt that she was being treated like a laboratory animal.

The creatures then left, but she was unable to free herself. Next, one of them came back and stuck a needle into her thigh, which paralysed her. He then proceeded to rape her. Because she had been immobilised she could not struggle, but she still felt the cold, clammy alien's every move. Afterwards, he pulled the needle out and the other creatures helped her down from the table. Then she collapsed.

When she awoke again she was standing by her car, fully dressed. In a state of turmoil, she got into the car and found that it worked perfectly well. Somehow she managed to drive home. Arriving at about 2.30am, she told her husband the whole story in floods of tears. They agreed to tell no one. However, four years later, in 1977, she met UFO investigator Barry King and decided to put her experiences on record.

Task accomplished

On the night of 3 March 1978, the 18-year-old José Alvaro was on his way over to his father's house in Fragata Pelotas, Brazil. His father was away and it was Alvaro's task to check that the house was secure.

Before he got there he was struck by a beam of blue light. Some time later, a passer-by saw him lying on the ground, as if he was in a drunken stupor. Alvaro awoke in a daze; images of war were racing through his brain, along with the phrase 'The task is accomplished'. Other witnesses had seen strange lights hovering in the area that night.

Under hypnosis, Alvaro recalled having been led into a room by an alien female with large eyes and silver hair. She forced him to have sex with her. There was another task that he would have to perform later, she said.

Strangely enough, before she knew of this Alvaro's mother had reported having had a strange dream, in which she was told that her son, who was unmarried, was about to become a father, but that the child would be born in another world.

Alien image from the 1960's.

Aliens in Scotland

On 17 August 1992, the painter and decorator Colin Wright and the mechanic Garry Wood were delivering a satellite dish to friend in a small village in West Lothian. At around 11.30pm they were rounding a bend in their vehicle when they saw a UFO hovering around 20 feet (6m) above the road, surrounded by a thin mist. As they drove under it a tube of light descended from the craft and suddenly everything went dark. The next thing that they knew they were skidding down the wrong side of the road at 70 miles (113km) an hour.

Both men felt high, and when they reached their friend's house they discovered that it was 1am: they had lost over an hour. Wright discovered that his safety belt was unbuckled, although he remembered doing it up at the start of the journey. The next day Wood began to suffer a series of headaches and Wright found that his eyes were sore.

Under hypnosis, Wood recalled seeing a floating examination table and a pool of gel, in which the aliens appeared to be living. He remembered one alien – a small 'grey', with large eyes – emerging from the goo. The creature appeared to be translucent and he could identify its skeleton and internal organs. He also saw a naked woman, who seemed cold and upset and certainly not as obliging as those who had descended to Earth in Latin America

Love bites?

Many abductees seem to end up with strange marks on their bodies. In the early hours of 29 November 1982 in Botucatu, Brazil, 38-year-old João Valeiro da Silva got out of bed for a drink of water. He was in the kitchen, he said, when he was hit by a beam of intense light, which he floated up into a UFO.

On board, he found himself surrounded by strange creatures. He was approached by a naked woman who touched his cheek, and it was at this point that he passed out. His family discovered him the next morning lying naked on the floor, with his clothes piled up next to him. His body was covered in strange marks and there were lesions on his penis, which, he said, he had never noticed before. Clearly an understanding soul, his wife put him to bed and nursed him better.

3 ◆ Making babies

One theory regarding alien abductions is that the aliens are trying to interbreed with humankind because they can have no offspring of their own. Some women abductees experience pregnancies that eventually mysteriously disappear; others are taken to see hybrid babies that they believe are their own.

The Birmingham baby

It is interesting that the alien abduction of Antônio Villas-Boas in 1957 occurred within days of the first artificial satellite, *Sputnik* I, orbiting the Earth (perhaps because humans invaded their world the aliens decided to get their own back). And it seems that aliens are not just entering the Earth's atmosphere because they want to have sex with earthlings: they want to impregnate human women, too. This sort of encounter appears to have happened first to an ordinary woman living in suburban Birmingham.

On 16 November 1957 the 27-year-old mother of two Cynthia Appleton suffered a 'missing-time' experience in her home at Fentham Road, Aston. Later she learnt that this was an alien attempt at contact that had failed. The aliens tried again, however. On 18 November, at 3pm, her front room was filled a rosy glow and the air was suffused with static electricity. It was then that an alien materialised, reeking of ozone. (A blackened newspaper indicated that there had been some sort of electrical discharge.)

The alien was tall, blond and perfectly proportioned – of the 'Nordic' type that is commonly seen in Britain. He wore the usual alien attire – a one-piece, silver jump suit – and communicated by means of telepathy. 'Do not be afraid', he said. They were soon locked in telepathic conversation. He came from the Gharnasvarn, he said, which Mrs Appleton took to mean Venus. The Gharnasvarnians apparently wanted to be friends with humans, but this was proving impossible because of humankind's aggressive nature and nuclear weapons. The alien illustrated what he was saying using three-dimensional images that he created in the air. (Holography was then in its infancy and it is unlikely that a Mrs Appleton would have known about it.) Although the alien showed Mrs Appleton a holographic image of his ship she never actually saw the craft.

The second time that he appeared he materialised inside the house again. After that, however, he arrived by more conventional means, turning up at the front door saying that he had driven there. Furthermore, as his exotic suit would have made him conspicuous, he took to wearing an ordinary cloth suit and a Homburg hat (which must have looked a little old-fashioned, even during the 1950s).

The alien visited her eight times in all. He seemed to have come in order to relate the secrets of the universe to her, because she was instructed on the structure of the atom, how to cure cancer and how to make a laser. (Although Albert Einstein had theoretically predicted the possibility of making lasers in 1917 the first working model was not built until 1960.) However, since she was not a professor of physics Mrs Appleton was not well equipped to absorb exactly what the alien was telling her. She asked why he had chosen to convey this information to the world via her and was told that it was because she had a brain that aliens could 'tune into'. For her part, Mrs Appleton found her selection something of a burden.

But worse was to come: in September 1958 the alien told her that she was going to have a baby which would 'belong to the race on Gharnas-varn'. He did not go into the details of how this would conceived, but when she went to the doctor she discovered that she was indeed pregnant. The child was furthermore born on the day that the alien had predicted; he had forecast its weight correctly, too, within an ounce. And the child also had fair hair.

A psychologist from Manchester interviewed Mrs Appleton and wrote up the case. She was also questioned by a priest, who found her to be a 'very trustworthy woman'. Her daughter said that she had seen the alien, too (but she was only four at the time). Apparently it also emerged that the alien had once burnt his hand and had given Mrs Appleton some salve to put on it; when she washed the wound a piece of skin had come off. Scientists at Birmingham and Manchester universities studied the skin but could not identify it, although they concluded that it was more like an animal's skin than a human's.

The lost love child

Elizabeth Klarer claimed that she had had numerous encounters with perfectly charming aliens between 1954 and 1963. Born in 1910, she had had a varied career, as a piano teacher, a meteorologist, a pilot and an intelligence officer in the South African Air Force. One of the extraterrestrials whom she had met was a handsome male humanoid, she said. She fell in love with him, but when she became pregnant she was whisked off to his home planet to have the child. She was then returned to Earth, but the aliens decreed that her baby had to stay behind. The planet may have been Clarion, from which the aliens that Truman Bethurum saw had supposedly come, because Klarer said that – like Clarion – it was free from war, poverty and disease and was therefore obviously the best place in which to bring up a child.

The mystery miscarriage

On the evening on 19 August 1979 36-year-old Lynda Jones was walking along the banks of the river Mersey, near Manchester, with her two children, aged 5 and 15. Suddenly the youngest shouted 'Mum, the moon is coming towards us'. Lynda looked up to see a huge, grey, Frisbee-shaped craft hurtling across the sky towards them. It came into view from behind some trees and she noticed some golfers playing on the greens as approached. 'It was not an optical illusion', she said. 'The object had a spinning effect and it seemed to be coming at us at an angle.'

For a moment she thought that it was a plane that was trying to make an emergency crash-landing at the nearby Manchester Airport. She pushed the children to the ground, telling them to lie flat and brace themselves. But there was no explosion, only silence. She saw the UFO pass slowly overhead. Then it dropped silently down behind the embankment that ran along the side of the river as a flood defence. The silence struck her more than anything else: 'It was more than just silence,' she said, 'it was complete stillness.' She realised that not only had there been no noise from the object, but there had also been no other sound either – neither bird song nor any traffic noise from the neighbouring motorway, which was always busy, day and night.

The UFO was now hidden behind the embankment. She wondered whether it had crashed and had then caught fire, so she ran up to the top of the embankment to take a look. Jones knew nothing about UFOs and what she saw amazed her: it was a crescent-shaped craft, 60 feet (18m) across and made from a fine network of metal. 'It looked so old-fashioned', she said. 'It really did look like something out of the Bible.'

The UFO hovered about 2 feet (60cm) above the ground and seemed to be constantly disappearing and reappearing. A light was somehow suspended from the underside of the craft. She was drawn towards it, and as she approached it became brighter. Then an orange ball of light appeared from the far side of the object. It rotated slowly and began to move menacingly in her direction. But she still continued to walk towards the spacecraft. 'Now it gives me the shivers', she recalled.

Suddenly her daughter screamed out 'Mum, come back. Come back.' The child's voice caused her to snap out of her trance and she simultaneously had a terrible premonition that it was Judgement Day.

Jones grabbed her children by the hand, turned on her heels and ran. Her five-year-old son was too small to keep up, so she swept him up into her arms and continued to flee. The spacecraft followed them and her terrified daughter looked back at it. 'Don't look back, just run', shouted Jones. The ground seemed to undulate beneath them. It was the strangest sight that she had ever seen, but they kept on running until they got home.

When they burst through the front door Jones' husband, Trevor, was home. He asked what the matter was with her eyes. When she looked in the mirror the skin beneath them was red and scaly. The fact that Trevor was home at all was even more peculiar. He usually worked until 10pm and did not get home until half-past. Jones had seen the UFO at around 9pm and the journey home would have taken only 10 minutes at walking pace. She had therefore lost nearly an hour. Jones said that she had got the impression that the UFO had made time slow down.

Afterwards, she found that her menstrual cycle had been disrupted and that there were marks on her body. Eighteen months later Jones underwent regressive hypnotism. Just before she had turned to run she recalled seeing an alien emerge from the UFO. She then had the feeling of floating before finding herself in a room with six small creatures of oriental appearance. They had slanting eyes, dark hair and yellow or olive skins. She had the feeling that she had seen one of them before. They laid her on a table and examined her. Bright lights were shone into her eyes, but the exact details of the examination were wiped from her mind.

Some weeks after the incident Jones noticed a waxy discharge from her vagina and her doctor told her that she had had a miscarriage, although she protested that she had not been pregnant. She was then sent to hospital to see a specialist, who found scar tissue on her Fallopian tubes of the type caused by an ectopic pregnancy – that is, when a fertilised egg develops in the Fallopian tube rather than in the womb. At first she could not account for this, but then she remembered another strange incident that had occurred one day in 1972 when she was out with Trevor. She had not seen a UFO on that occasion, but when they pieced the events of the day together they seemed to have lost six hours in 'missing time'.

Wise baby

In the summer of 1979 a Cheshire woman heard a strange, humming sound and looked up to see a UFO. Soon afterwards she unexpectedly became pregnant. The pregnancy sparked a series of bizarre dreams, in which she gave birth to an incredibly ugly, but frighteningly intelligent, child. (In the terminology of ufology this type of child is known as a 'wise baby'.) These dreams scared her so much that when she miscarried three months into the pregnancy she was profoundly relieved.

But that was not the end of the story. Five years after her original sighting she was awoken during the night by the same humming sound. She then saw a tall, blonde female, with blue eyes, in her bedroom, who effortlessly floated her out of the bedroom window.

She had little further memory of the incident and did not undergo regressive hypnosis. However, she did know that she had been examined and also had the sneaking feeling that something 'very important' had happened.

Three years later, she was again awoken during the night by what she believed was the hand of a three-year-old child holding her own. She cried out and her husband switched on the light. As he did so, a ball of light flew out of the bedroom.

Holding the baby

In 1988 Barbara Archer was a 21-year-old university student who was studying to become a journalist when she became plagued by feelings of fear and anxiety. She began to experience strange flashbacks of bizarre events in her life of which she had no memory, so she therefore sought professional advice.

Under hypnosis, she recalled an experience that had happened to her when she was 16. She had been getting ready for bed one night when she noticed a light shining in through the window. She closed the curtains, but the light still seemed to illuminate the whole room. She peeked out of the window but could see no source for the light. She looked out of the other window, too, and then felt the strange sensation that there was someone in the room with her.

She saw a small creature by the wardrobe, which she took to be male. Although she was puzzled by the light, she was not shocked to see him there. He touched her on the wrist, which reassured her. Then she began to float out of the window; she said that it was like being in a lift with no walls. She could clearly see first the driveway, and then her house, then the rest of street below her. She was scared of heights and her levitation made her feel nauseous; she hoped that she would not be sick.

She floated upwards until she was underneath some sort of flying saucer. It was dark grey and metallic. Then she noticed that the light that she had seen was coming out of it. The alien whom she had noticed in her bedroom was still with her. More were waiting inside.

She also recalled having been abducted when she was 12. That time she had found herself in a room containing 40 or 50 tables. After she had been subjected to a physical examination a tall alien had come over to her and had looked deep into her mind. This made her feel happy and she lay back and relaxed; she did not feel sick, just a little cold. Although she was scared of the smaller aliens, she liked the taller one and thought that he liked her, too. There was a very sexual element to this feeling and although she was only 12 Archer suddenly felt very womanly, very grown up. She got the feeling that the alien could read her mind and really understood her.

She remembered that she had also been abducted at the age of 16, when she was suffering from anorexia, which had annoyed the aliens because she had stopped menstruating.

When she was 21, Archer went on holiday to Ireland, from where she was yet again abducted. This time the aliens had become cross with her because she had not taken off her clothes quickly enough. Later she had been taken to a nursery on board the spacecraft, where there were about 20 babies in cribs. Some were in nappies; others were slightly older and were dressed in simple smocks. They all looked rather odd because they did not have much hair and because their skin was an unnatural, grey colour.

The aliens had told her that she could hold one, and had picked out a baby girl for her. The child had had big eyes, which were shaped like an alien's but were not as ugly. Archer remembered feeling very protective and maternal. The alien nurse had then told her to feed it and she had obediently put the baby to her breast. Afterwards they had taken the baby away from her. When Archer was told that she had to leave she had felt bad about leaving the baby behind. She had asked the aliens whether she could see it again, but they did not give her an answer.

A non-maternal abductee

In 1957 the nine-year-old Jill Pinzarro was returning home from the library on her bike when she decided to take a short cut through the park. It was years later, when she was a minister, that she revealed what happened next.

She had stopped by a bench, parked her bike and sat down to do some reading. There was still an hour to go before dinner. Then she wandered into the nearby wood, but did not know why. Suddenly she felt the presence of someone beside her before seeing a strange glow. She walked towards it and found herself standing under something. She noticed a ladder and climbed up it into an alien spacecraft, where she was stripped and examined.

When she returned to the park bench it was already dark. Scared, she put her books in the basket into her bike and set off for home. It was late and her parents were frantic; they had already called the police, who were out looking for her. But when she arrived at her house her parents were so relieved that they were not even angry with her.

She was 11 when she was next abducted, the aliens being particularly interested in the scab on her knee – the result of falling off her bike. A tall alien stared into her eyes, which she found reassuring: the alien, she thought, really cared about her and would not let her come to any harm. This feeling was not initially accompanied by any sexual sensations and she thought that the alien was a female. However, when the alien touched her on the forehead, she felt calm and was willing to surrender sexually to the creature.

When she was abducted in 1980, at the age of 32, she was given a baby to hold. It was about two and a half months old, she reckoned, and had little hair and light skin. The alien nursemaid said that the child needed nurturing, but that they were not very good at it and therefore needed her to do it. The baby was quiet and seemed to enjoy Pinzarro holding it. When she had to give it back she felt an acute sense of loss. She had bonded with it, but thought that this was strange because she did not consider herself to be a very maternal person. She had only ever wanted one child, which, indeed, she had – back on Earth.

Abducting embryos

Lynn Miller, a Mennonite woman who worked as a waitress, had been the victim of numerous inexplicable events for all of her life. But things began to make sense in 1986, when she was 31. She was driving to Cape May, New Jersey, with her son, when she saw a huge UFO hovering above the road near Tuckahoe. She stopped the car and was promptly abducted.

Separated from her son, she was forced to strip and climb onto an examination table. A tall alien then looked into her eyes and placed his hands on her head. She felt an overwhelming surge of love for him; there was a strong sexual element to this, a feeling of pleasure. Then the alien conducted a gynaecological examination on her. The aliens next poked a long needle into her womb through her navel/. It hurt, but the aliens put their hands on her head, which took the pain away. The aliens told her that they were implanting something in her, but did not say what.

Some time later, she was abducted again, and this time and a long, black instrument that looked like a speculum was pushed into her to dilate her vagina. It had suction cup on it and was attached to some sort of machine. She felt a tearing sensation inside her and complained to the tall alien who was performing the operation that they were hurting her, but they continued anyway. The tall alien then pulled something out of her and put it into a fluid-filled container that was handed to him by a smaller creature. They showed it to her and she recognised it as being a foetus. The tall alien told her that it was her child and that they were going to raise it. She protested that they had no right to do so, but the alien took no notice and placed the foetus into an incubator before telling her to get dressed.

The aliens also took her into another room, where they showed her a chart and told her to memorise the names inscribed on it. Miller was puzzled by this, but an alien told her that it would help them. When she wondered why they needed help, the alien explained that there was a war on and she needed to know these names. Although she looked at the chart she made no active effort to remember the information on it. However, the alien moved close to her and she got the impression that he was telepathically storing the names in her memory.

The next thing that she remembered was that she was again on Earth, miles from where she had stopped, in a part of New Jersey that she did not recognise. She got back into her car and drove home. Two hours were missing from her memory of events.

She additionally recalled having been abducted when she was six.

Artists impression
of visitors from
another planet

Being a Mennonite, she was not allowed to have vaccinations and consequently came down with diphtheria. For religious reasons, too, her mother would not permit her to be taken to hospital; the doctor visited her every day, but there was little that he could do. Miller's condition deteriorated steadily for two weeks until it reached the point at which the doctor did not expect her to survive the night. But the next morning her mother discovered her playing happily on the floor. The doctor was called and found that her temperature had returned to normal and that the symptoms of diphtheria had varnished.

During the night, Miller remembered, she had been abducted by aliens. They had told her that they had come to cure her. They wound a tube around her body and made her stand in a strange machine. The aliens then sat around her in chairs and watched as a curtain of blue light descended from the top of the machine. Afterwards she was told that she had been 'cleansed'. The disease was certainly gone and although the doctor ordered her back to bed for another week it was a struggle to keep her there: all she could think about was getting up and playing.

Siring aliens

James Austino was a student at Temple University, Philadelphia, when he came to the conclusion that the strange events that had plagued him throughout his life might be due to alien abduction. Fortunately for Austino, the distinguished ufologist David M Jacobs was also working at Temple University, where he was conducting research into the alien-abduction phenomenon, so Austino underwent regressive hypnosis with Jacobs.

He remembered that in 1980, when he was 14, he had been with his girlfriend, Monique, when the aliens came to get him. Monique was 'switched off' and Austino alone was taken. He next remembered lying on a table, which had a bright light above it. An alien pulled it down, over his groin area, before starting to fumble around. Austino found this a bit embarrassing, but something in his mind kept telling him that it was alright. The alien seemed to being showing his genitals to a colleague.

Austino asked what was happening and the alien then put his face close to his and implanted in his mind an image of the naked Monique. He got an erection, whereupon they attached his penis to a machine and took a sample of his semen.

(In this case there was no witness to the procedure, but some female abductees claim to have seen semen samples being taken from their boyfriends if they were abducted along with them. And one poor mother witnessed aliens taking a semen sample from her teenage son. Luckier abductees report having been bonded to female aliens and getting the impression that they were making love to a human female.)

Next, Austino was shown what his semen would be used for. The aliens took him to a room that was full of incubators, which looked like fish tanks with tubes coming out of them and were illuminated by a strange, blue light. There were 60 or 70 of them. He was allowed to inspect them more closely and saw that there were foetuses inside. They looked like little bald hamsters with black eyes, he said. The foetuses floated in a liquid that gurgled and bubbled, and they had wires attached to them. As far as Austino could tell, they were human foetuses, although their eyes were very different.

He was abducted again when he was 21, when he was given a mind scan. Then, when he was 23, he was abducted for a third time and saw a young woman wearing a white smock who was helping the aliens. She took a dip in a large, oval pool containing a luminous-green liquid and urged him to join her. So he jumped in; the pool was about 5 feet (1.5m) deep. The aliens who were watching looked pleased.

The woman encouraged Austino to lie back and relax. On doing so, he sank to the bottom, but found that he could still breathe. The woman then got out, whereupon he began to feel numb and almost blacked out. He therefore pushed himself up and two aliens helped him to get out of the pool. He observed that the liquid did not run off his body like water: it was more viscous and had to be slopped off by hand.

Paternal instinct

In 1989 the 34-year-old alcohol-rehabilitation counsellor Andrew Garcia was abducted. After having his mind scanned he was introduced to a five-year-old girl who looked like his niece, only with big, black eyes.

She looked deep into his own eyes, which evoked all sorts of intense emotion in him: he wanted to hold the child and love her. She touched him, but then pulled back, which upset him. He did not want her to leave. The aliens who were watching did not understand this and studied his emotional reaction intensely. A tall alien then stared into his eyes, whereupon Garcia calmed down. 'This is how it has to be', he was told. The alien said that he could see the child again another time.

4 ❖ Abductions in mind

Aliens also seem to take a great interest in human minds, as well as their bodies. Many abductees report that they have had their minds scanned by alien creatures. Abductions often have a spooky, psychic dimension to them and sometimes leave victims with permanently enhanced mental powers.

I met a man who wasn't there

Maureen Puddy, a 27-year-old mother from the Australian town of Rye, had an invalid husband and two young children when, in June 1972, her seven-year-old son was involved in an accident. His leg was injured and he was taken by air ambulance to a hospital in Heidelberg, near Melbourne.

On the night of 5 July 1972 she was driving down the Mooraduc Road on her way to visit the boy in hospital. Between the towns of Frankston and Dromana she spotted a blue light in the sky that seemed to be following her. She initially thought that it could have been an air ambulance, so she stopped to take a look, but when she got out of the car she saw that it was no helicopter. It was a giant UFO, shaped like two saucers, one above the other, around 100 feet (30m) in diameter. It made a low, humming sound, glowed all over with a blue light and hovered just 40 feet (12m) above the ground. Mrs Puddy got back into her car and drove off. The UFO followed her and chased her for 30 miles (48km) down the deserted road before suddenly peeling away and shooting off like a streak of light into the distance. She reported to the matter to the local police.

On 25 July 1972, driving down the same stretch of road at 9.15 at night, Mrs Puddy saw the UFO again. But this time the car's engine died on her when she tried to escape. Out of her control, the car was dragged onto the grass verge and the UFO now appeared to hover directly over it. Mrs Puddy was bathed in blue light and felt as if she was in the centre of a vacuum.

It was then that she felt a telepathic communication being beamed down to her. The voice that she heard in her head, she said, sounded like it was translating what it had to say from a foreign tongue. The voice said

'All your tests will be negative'. Mrs Puddy had no idea what this was supposed to mean. Then it said 'Tell the media, do not panic, we mean no
harm'. And finally: 'You now have control.'

The car now roared back to life. The eerie, blue glow and the strange,
vacuum effect disappeared and Mrs Puddy sped off. She went straight to
the police again, who this time put her in touch with the Royal Australian
Air Force. It checked its records, but could identify no unusual aircraft
movements in the area on that night, and then told her to say nothing to
anyone. However, Mrs Puddy did contact Judith Magee, of the Victoria
UFO Research Society.

Magee revealed that there had been some other peculiar sightings in
the sky in the area on that night: 21-year-old engineering manager Maris
Ezergailis had reported seeing a blue streak of light in the sky from nearby
Mount Waverley. 'It was like a meteor trail, but an unusually broad one,
travelling horizontally', he said.

When Mrs Puddy heard of this she became excited. She had seen a
broad, blue streak of light just like that when the UFO had shot off after her
first encounter with it. The problem was that Ezergailis had observed the
streak at 10pm, so if he had seen the UFO streaking off Mrs Puddy had lost
45 minutes during her encounter.

Mrs Puddy was worried by the aliens' instruction to 'tell the media'.
She feared that the aliens would come back again if she did not do what
they said. They did. On 22 February 1973 Mrs Puddy was doing the house-
work when she heard a voice. It said 'Maureen, come to the meeting place'.
At first she thought that there was someone at the door, but throughout the
day she heard the voice over and over again. Eventually she came to the
conclusion that the aliens were telepathically planting the voice into her
head. It was thus plain that the aliens wanted to talk to her again.

She called Magee, who agreed to meet her, along with her fellow UFO-
investigator Paul Norman, out on the Mooraduc Road at 8.30pm. When
Mrs Puddy arrived she was flustered, and claimed nearly to have been run
off the road. Magee calmed her down and asked her to drive them back to
the place where the incident had occurred. When Magee got into Mrs
Puddy's car she felt a tingling sensation, 'like a mild electric shock'.

On the way, Mrs Puddy explained to the two investigators that a figure
wearing a gold suit had materialised inside the car, between the two front
seats, before disappearing again. When they reached the spot where she
said that this had happened she claimed that she could see it again, this

time standing outside the car. Magee and Norman could see nothing. Norman even got out of the car and stood on the exact spot where Mrs Puddy claimed that she could see the figure. Mrs Puddy said the figure had stepped backwards to let Norman by.

Mrs Puddy then said that the figure had gestured to her that she should follow him. Magee volunteered to go, too, but Mrs Puddy gripped the steering wheel hard and replied that she would go nowhere. It was then that Mrs Puddy announced that she was being abducted. While the startled UFO investigators looked on, Mrs Puddy began describing the inside of the UFO, whose crew, she asserted, had kidnapped her. 'I can't get out', she yelled. 'There are no doors or windows.' She saw a strange 'mushroom' in the room. Inside it it looked like jelly was moving about. 'He wants me to close my eyes', she said. Then she fell into a hypnotic trance and continued describing what she saw inside the ship. Fortunately, the trance-like state did not last very long. 'He's gone', said Mrs Puddy, coming round. 'I can tell. It feels different.'

Magee wrote up the case for *Flying Saucer Review* only a few weeks after the event. Although Mrs Puddy had not physically gone anywhere during the abduction, there was one that Judith Magee was convinced of: she had not been making it up and had been genuinely upset by her experience.

A meeting of minds

Vaunda Hoscik was first abducted by aliens when she was 14. Since then it had happened to her hundreds more times. Although she believed that they were conducting regular tests on her, she thought that she was benefiting from her contact with them, too.

Hoscik was born in 1975, in south London. Of eastern European extraction, she believed herself to be psychic. In 1989 she went to bed one night at 10pm; after over four hours of peaceful sleep she woke suddenly 2.45am. She sat up in bed, but then found herself overcome by a creeping paralysis. Only her eyes were unaffected. She was suddenly pushed back onto the bed with considerable force. There were four grey, foetus-like figures in the room. They had dark, slanted eyes and were about 4 feet (1.2m) tall, with long, thin arms. She tried to scream, but found that she could not do so.

The next thing that she knew she was in a brightly lit room surrounded by computer screens. The room also contained a number of tables on which other humans were lying. She was scared and confused, but one of the aliens then telepathically reassured her, telling her not to worry because they wanted to help her. She was subjected to a number of psychological tests involving numbers and shapes. Then she found herself in her bedroom. She had been gone for three-quarters of an hour.

On the following night the aliens came for her again and conducted a series of tests on her. Their telepathic instructions were so clear that she got the impression that they were talking to her rather than implanting their thoughts directly into her mind. However, she sometimes found that they were going too fast and therefore begged them to slow down.

The aliens told her that they came from Zeta Reticuli (which is where Betty Hill's Star Map indicated that her aliens were from). They said that they abducted a lot of humans for testing, but usually chose those with psychic powers. To the aliens, humans were primitive creatures. They themselves had evolved far beyond humankind, but had lost their emotions due to cloning. They would be happy to exchange some of their advanced technology in order to get them back.

Hoscik was a secretive child and told no one of her multiple abductions. Her father was ill and her mother worked long hours to support the family. They did not notice that their daughter was disappearing in the middle of the night, even though she claimed that at one time she was abducted every night for 18 months. She explained that she did not tell anyone about her abductions because she was afraid that she would be called a liar. However, she had devised a plan with which to prove that she had been abducted by aliens. On one occasion she had taken book with her to show the aliens, hoping thereby to discover whether she could carry things to the spacecraft and back. When she found that she could she bought herself a camera and one night took some surreptitious photographs of the aliens at work. When she took the film to be developed, however, the pictures did not come out properly. Realising that she was now out of pocket, the aliens kindly left the exact amount that she had spent on the camera, film and developing under her pillow.

Hoscik believed that the aliens benefited her as much as she helped them: while she taught them about feelings they boosted her intellect. Soon she was overachieving at school, which caused her problems because she began to be bullied. In order to stop this, she consciously began underachieving. This strategy had the added advantage of discouraging her nocturnal visitors, who did not appear when she was not being intellectually stimulated.

After leaving school she drifted from job to job. Like many alien abductees, she was unsettled and aimless. Eventually the abductions ceased altogether. Then, in 1995, she met Chris Martin. She knew that he was someone special because six years before the pair met the aliens had shown her a picture of him. Martin was a UFO enthusiast and a science-fiction buff. He asked her whether anything strange had ever happened to her. She said that it had and, for the first time in her life, admitted to being an abductee.

Martin wanted her to resume contact with the aliens, and she knew how to. Together they went back to the house in which she had been brought up. They took some intelligence tests with them. Martin was amazed at how quickly she got through them. This intense intellectual stimulation in turn attracted the aliens. But this time they did not abduct her, simply establishing remote telepathic communication with her and using her to channel alien information to Earth.

A number of aliens whom Hoscik called 'grey twos' channelled through her. She named them Antholas, Minnie and Crispin because she could neither remember nor pronounce their real names. Antholas told her that there were 16 different types of alien besieging the Earth. Although some of them were experimenting on humans, he said, they were also afraid that humans would conduct experiments on them, which was why they revealed themselves in such a covert fashion. The aliens reckoned that one in ten humans believed in them; when everyone was convinced of their existence then they might learn to trust humankind enough to reveal themselves fully. They abducted people so that they could get to know them on a personal level, after which those individuals would spread the word of their existence. At the same time, Antholas said, they were trying to extend the capacity of the human brain as much as possible, in order to enable humankind to approach their own level of learning.

Minnie was a younger alien who had been entrusted to Hoscik for the sake of her emotional education. Older aliens told Hoscik that Minnie was her child, who had been fathered by an alien. At first, Hoscik refused to accept this, but then came to believe that she did indeed have a hybrid child which had been taken from her. She consequently severed all contact with the aliens, destroyed all records of her communications with them and also broke up with Martin.

A family tormented

British UFO investigator Tony Dodd was approached by Darren and Tracey Jones, a young couple with four children, in 1997. Tracey was psychic. From childhood she had had the sensation that she was being watched and she also had a phobia about being grabbed by unseen hands in the dark.

The family had been bothered by odd, abduction-related events for years. In 1993 they were living in a cottage in Yorkshire. One evening, at around 9pm, they had heard a strange, humming noise coming from outside. Suddenly the cottage was bathed in light. The experience seemed to last only for a few seconds, although the clock said that a quarter of an hour had passed. The following morning they found that the padlocks on the stable doors had been forced and that the wrought-iron front gate had been buckled and twisted.

Tracey had had a chest operation. The wound had become badly infected and she wore a bandage that had to be changed daily. One morning she awoke to find that the bandage was gone; they could not find it anywhere. But the pain from the wound had also vanished – as had the infection. On another night the underwear that she had been wearing underneath her pyjamas similarly went missing and never turned up.

They began to think that the house was haunted. Darren saw strange figures in the night. Other inexplicable things also happened and the electrical appliances and plumbing system in the house seemed to have a mind of their own. No one else who had lived in the house previously had reported experiencing such occurrences, however.

When the Jones family moved to another old house, overlooking the Yorkshire moors, they were plagued by UFO sightings and bizarre, 'missing-time' experiences. Two-year-old Marcus began having nightmares. Tracey saw strange men in monks' habits standing at the end of her bed and awoke during the night to find herself paralysed. In the morning, though, she was perfectly fit, except for the strange marks that she and the rest of the family developed on their bodies: they were bruises that looked like finger marks.

In 1997 Darren got a job in Dubai and initially went out there alone. It was a peaceful time for them, with no odd occurrences. But when Tracey and the rest of the family arrived in Dubai everything became as crazy as before. The electrical appliances again went haywire and the family had more 'missing-time' experiences. Marcus had the idea that he could fly; he said that a man lived in his bedroom light and took him and his sister, Georgina, up into the light to play. One night Georgina saw a small man surrounded by light standing at the foot of her bed. The following day she had finger marks on her body. When she drew the man whom she had seen, Marcus recognised him as being the man who lived in the light. By now the man had become malevolent, however, and after Marcus complained that the man was hurting his tummy he had to sleep in his parents' bedroom.

After they returned to Yorkshire the man in the light continued to bother Marcus. The youngest child then began having nightmares, which became associated with the marks that were now being found on his body, too. Strange things happened around the house and whole family heard unexplained bangs during the night, as well as unfamiliar strange voices; Tracey thought that she recognised the voice of a stillborn child that she had lost years before.

Like many women abductees, Tracey suffered from nosebleeds. Under hypnosis, she recalled that the two men that she had seen wearing monks' habits had taken her to a round room, where she lay on a bed, unable to move even though nothing seemed to be restraining her. A strange apparatus was being used to operate on her chest.

Dodd believed that Tracey – and probably also the rest of the family – had been abducted many times, but put his investigation on hold until the children were old enough to undergo regressive hypnosis.

Psychic connections

Luli Oswald was the stage name of the Brazilian concert pianist Margarida Henriquieta Marchesini. The mother of seven and a charity worker, she was also a well-known psychic.

On the evening of 15 October 1979 she was driving from Rio de Janeiro to Saquarema with a 25-year-old male student. It had been raining earlier, but by then it was about 9.30pm and the skies had cleared. As they drove along the coastal road the topic of UFOs came up in conversation and Oswald asked the young man what he would do if he saw one. At that moment they noticed a dome-shaped object, with three lights on it, out to sea. It could not be a UFO, Oswald thought – that would be just too coincidental. But the lights were keeping apace with them, so, in order to be on the safe side, they turned off the coastal road with the intention of following an inland route. However, once in the hinterland they lost their way.

People watch as a UFO flies overhead.

The student, who was driving, took a wrong turning and they found themselves on the coastal road again. Once on it, they had no sensible option but to continue.

By now it was about 11.30pm and they were in a hurry to get home. Suddenly they saw the lights again: this time they were rising out of the sea, pulling a huge column of water with them. At that point the car's engine cut out. They were terrified, but worse was to come. Above them, on the cliff tops, was another UFO – this one was long and pencil shaped, with orange windows along its side. It sent three balls of dazzling, white light hurtling down the cliffs towards them. They panicked and were unable to decide whether they would be safer in the car or taking shelter underneath it. It made no difference, because they both blacked out.

The next thing that they knew the danger had passed. They were still in the car, but it was now in a side road leading to a farm a little further down the main highway. They set off again, both of them feeling the need for something with which to settle their nerves. Oswald knew of a petrol station that sold coffee; when they got there, however, it was shut. It was already 2am.

Oswald experienced some bad after-effects following that night. Her eyes burnt for a couple of days. She was unable to pass water, and when she finally did she felt a burning sensation. There was something wrong with her watch, too: it gained minutes every day, rendering it virtually useless. Unsettled, she went to her local priest, who put her in touch with the Brazilian UFO investigator Irene Granchi. A US ufologist was also visiting Brazil at the time, and he checked out the Fiat 147 that they had been driving. It was heavily magnetised down one side. Oswald then agreed to undergo regressive hypnosis.

Under hypnosis, she remembered that they had come face to face with the UFO. It had bathed the car in a beam of light, which had lifted the vehicle off the ground and had pulled it into the spaceship. She next recalled being in room, surrounded by ugly creatures who were 4 feet 6 inches (1.35m) tall, with grey skins, pointed features and long, thin arms. They removed her clothes and examined her, using strange lights whose beams hurt her eyes. They then took samples of her hair and gave her a complete gynaecological examination. However, they telepathically told her that she was of no physical use to them (perhaps because she was then past child-bearing age); she had been chosen, they said, because she was psychic. For the purposes of their research they were interested only in the young man. She saw him lying unconscious on a table; the aliens were examining his sexual organs and taking samples of his semen.

The aliens then volunteered a curious piece of information: they told her that they were from a 'small galaxy near Neptune'. Oswald was an educated woman and knew that this made no sense – to a human mind, at least.

Tall ships

On 15 August 1992 the transatlantic businessman Harry, along with Janet, a computer-banking executive, went to see the tall-ships' parade at the Albert Dock in Liverpool. After that they went back to Janet's flat, where they spent the night together.

At around 3am Janet awoke in a state of absolute terror. She was convinced that she had not had a nightmare, but had actually been somewhere in her sleep; the moment before she woke up she had had the sensation that she had been placed back into bed. Janet woke Harry, who thought that he saw something in the bedroom.

Janet gradually began to recover some memories of what had happened. She remembered lying down in a brilliantly lit room. They were a number of creatures standing around her. (She could not picture their faces and believed that her mind was somehow blocking out the details.) The beings gave her something to calm her down, which paralysed her. After that they started to do something to her – she did not know exactly what – which she did not like.

The next incident that she recalled was being in a room with a strange man who had compelling eyes. He seemed very knowledgeable and began telling her things. She could not remember precisely what, but had the strange sensation that he had talked to her before.

Then she found herself in a corridor with a man whom she had known when she was 12. He had been very bright in those days, but now appeared demented. She was taken into the room that he had just left and was terrified that she might come out of it in the same state as him. She was reassured, however, to see a human being in the room who seemed to be a kindly doctor. He explained that they were going to have to operate on her in order to put something right. She put up a fight, but the next thing that she remembered was being back in bed.

Janet was convinced that she had conceived a baby that night. She had been trying to become pregnant for some time, but without success until them. She also came down with all sorts of strange ailments, including headaches, lethargy, sore eyes and blocked sinuses. For his part, Harry had a strange mark on his leg, which quickly faded.

One night both Janet and Harry dreamt that when they had been watching the tall ships on the quay they had been beamed up into a flying saucer, which then flew off. In the morning they ran to the bathroom and vomited.

Janet's ill-health persisted until, on her doctor's advice, she had the pregnancy terminated, whereupon she quickly got better. Then, on 15 November 1992, she again awoke at 3am. Three of the creatures whom she had seen during the original incident were in the bedroom. She tried to scream, but could make no sound. She believed that the aliens were angry with her because she had aborted the baby.

Under regressive hypnosis, Janet recalled having seen small, hairless 'playmates' in her room when she was a child. They had scared her. She also remembered having flown up to a special 'playroom', which had taken her to the places that she wanted to visit. She had furthermore been shown pictures of the Earth and had been told that it was in danger. Other pieces of wisdom had been imparted to her either from boxes or from a tall man, with whom she had been left alone and who had implanted something into her, she believed. Both she and her mother had suffered from terrible nosebleeds, which had persisted during Janet's life. She also told of 'missing-time' experiences, which also seemed to have affected her brother and his girlfriend.

Harry had seen a UFO once, he said. He had also had a vivid dream about being strapped down onto a table and being examined; he had felt his head being cut open. He later saw a girl whom he recognised from his class at school being operated on.

Both Janet and Harry said that they had been followed by 'men in black' (who often appear to witnesses or victims of alien abductions).

The Swedish experience
On 23 March 1974 a man named Anders left a political celebration in Vallentuna, Sweden, and set off to walk home to Lindholmen, a distance of about 3 miles (4.8km). He had had a few drinks, but claimed that he was still sober.

It was a moonlit night and he decided to take a short cut over a hill. As he neared the peak he saw a light coming towards him; thinking that it was a fast-moving car, he leapt off the road. He slipped down the embankment and landed on the grass at the bottom. When he looked up, he realised that what he had seen was not a car at all. The light was hovering directly above him.

The next thing that he remembered, he was outside his own front door. His wife answered his frantic ringing of the doorbell and found him bleeding from a wound on his forehead. His cheeks were also burnt.

The next day, he called the Swedish ministry of defence, which put him in touch with a UFO investigator. Under hypnosis, Anders recalled that when he had flung himself from the road he had not actually hit the ground – some unseen force had lifted him into the air and had transported upwards, into a spaceship. The craft had been manned by four 'semi-transparent' aliens. They had the features of Indians, he said, although they possessed no noses or ears. In fact, they could have been wearing hoods, he thought. Anyway, they were surrounded by an eerie glow. They had approached him with an instrument that he did not like the look of. He had tried to fight them off, but they had overpowered him and had placed the instrument against his forehead, whereupon he had experienced a burning sensation. Then they had dropped him off outside his home.

In this case there was no missing time, but a woman cyclist had seen a strange light at the time that Anders said that he had been abducted, as had a courting couple who were out for a drive. They thought that it was a light shining from the window of a water tower, but there was no water tower in the vicinity. On the following night more strange lights appeared in the sky. People watching television reported interference; there was also something wrong with the phones.

In common with other abductees, his experience subsequently gave Anders the sensation of 'oneness with the world'. He felt a pricking feeling inside his head, too – at the spot where the aliens had placed the instrument – and suspected that they had implanted something inside his brain. Anders furthermore began to exhibit paranormal talents. He was sensitive to magnets located 1 foot (30cm) away, while rock crystal placed at a distance of 6 or 7 feet (1.8 or 2.1m) from him elicited a sucking feeling in his head.

A year after his abduction Anders had a dream, in which he was told to 'search in yttrium'. Anders thought that yttrium was a place; it is, however, a rare metal that is used as a component in colour television screens. UFO investigators discovered that Anders was sensitive to yttrium, especially along certain notional lines within his body that were similar to those delineated in acupuncture charts.

One of Anders' new psychical abilities was the ability to dowse. He accordingly dowsed the abduction site and discovered that a number of ley lines converged on it. When a chart recording Anders' biorhythms was analysed it was found that he had been abducted at the exact moment when his three fundamental energies – emotional, intellectual and physical

– had peaked simultaneously. This triple maximum is believed to occur only once every 46 years.

A change for the better

On 27 October 1974 the 28-year-old John and the 25-year-old Sue Day were driving home to Aveley, in Essex, after having visited relatives in east London. Their three children were dozing in the back of the car.

At around 10.20pm, when they were not far from Aveley, they spotted a blue light in the sky which appeared to be following them. The car radio then packed up and began giving off smoke, so John pulled out the wires that connected it to the car. As they rounded a bend they entered a patch of strange, green mist and the car was jolted quite violently. When they emerged from the mist they found that they were much further down the road than they had expected. On arriving home they switched on the TV, only to find that the evening's programmes had finished. They had somehow lost several hours during their journey.

When the Days' case came to the attention of the ufologists Barry King and Andy Collins they decided to investigate it using regressive hypnosis – the first time that the technique had been used in Britain. Under hypnosis, Sue revealed that the family had been 'drawn out' of the car into a spaceship. But strangely enough, as she looked down she could still see herself and the others sitting in the vehicle. Their abductors were tall, fair humanoids wearing silver suits and 'Balaclava helmets'. (These so-called 'Nordics' feature regularly in British UFO abductions.) With them were smaller creatures with bat-like faces, who were trained 'examiners', she said.

Sue recalled that the Days had undergone medical examinations at the hands of their abductors. Then John had been shown the engine room and they had all watched a holographic film of the aliens' home planet, which seemed a rather gloomy place. The aliens said that the human race was the result of a genetic experiment that they were conducting and that they came to Earth every so often in order to check on their progress. The aliens had next planted orders to perform certain tasks in the family members' unconscious minds and had then wiped their memories.

The hypnosis sessions were terminated because some of those present thought that Sue was responding directly to the questions that were being asked rather than reporting what she was seeing and hearing while in her regressed state.

However, during the three years that had elapsed between the abduction and the hypnosis sessions the Days' family life had undeniably changed radically. They had all become vegetarians and passionate environmentalists. John had developed numerous artistic skills and was about to change his job. And they all reported a number of psychic experiences.

5 ✦ Abductions USA

The stories that have appeared in books, films and magazines seem to have made the USA the alien-abduction capital of the world. Is this because the Americans are more open-minded than any other nationality? Are they more eager to talk about being abducted? Or is it because there are more media to report their claims than in any other country?

A fishing trip

The 18-year-old Calvin Parker and the 45-year-old Charles Hickson were fishing from a disused pier on the Pascagoula river, in Mississippi, on 11 October 1973. First they heard a strange, buzzing sound and then they saw an egg-shaped spacecraft 10 feet (3m) wide and 8 feet (2.4m) high that was emitting an eerie, bluish-white glow and was hovering above the river some 40 feet (12m) from the bank.

The craft landed and three aliens floated out (they had legs, but did not use them). The creatures were about 5 feet (1.5m) tall, with odd, conical protrusions instead of ears and noses and slits where their mouths would have been. They had claws for hands and horrible, grey, wrinkled skin (although the two men said that this may have been a uniform).

Two of them grabbed Hickson and the third seized Parker, who fainted. The two humans were then taken aboard the spacecraft, where Hickson was given some sort of medical examination, which involved being scanned by what seemed to be a large eye that floated in mid-air. Hickson was consequently paralysed, except for his eyes. Parker, he assumed, was being examined elsewhere. After about 20 minutes Hickson was dumped unceremoniously back on the pier, where he found Parker crying and praying nearby. Then the craft rose up vertically and shot out of sight.

At first Hickson and Parker kept quiet about their abduction, being afraid that they would attract ridicule. Then they decided that the government ought to know about it and accordingly called Kessler Air Force Base in Biloxi; a sergeant there told them to speak to their local sheriff. After going to the local newspaper's office, which they found closed, they went directly to the sheriff's office to report the abduction. They both gave a detailed description of the incident to the sheriff, Fred Diamond, without being hypnotised. Diamond then left them alone in his office for some time and eavesdropped on them via a hidden microphone, thinking that if they were hoaxers they would use the opportunity to go over their story together once again, or else to have a laugh at the sheriff's expense. Instead, however, he heard Parker praying and then telling Hickson that he wanted to see a doctor. Hickson himself was evidently awe-struck by the power of the craft that he had seen. Neither gave any hint that they did not believe everything that they had reported. 'If they were lying they should be in Hollywood', said Diamond later.

The two were subsequently subjected to lie-detector tests conducted by the Pendleton Detective Agency in New Orleans. The sceptical machine operator, Scott Glasgow, was determined to prove that they were lying. Instead, however, they easily passed. 'This son of a bitch is telling the truth', Glasgow exclaimed afterwards.

They were also interviewed at Kessler Air Force Base and their case was investigated by Dr J Allen Hynek, of the USAF's Project Blue Book, too. Hickson submitted himself to regressive hypnosis under Professor James A Harder, of the University of California, but the session had to be stopped when Hickson became too distressed to continue. He nevertheless handled the aftermath of the abduction well; by contrast, Parker had a nervous breakdown and required psychiatric care. 'I had to learn to accept what had happened', said Hickson. 'I saw what happened to a man who could not accept it. This thing almost destroyed his life.'

Unlike other abductees, Hickson did not write a book about the incident, nor did he try to exploit his experience in any way. 'I had a chance to make a million dollars', he explained. 'I was offered all kinds of money to let them do a movie. I declined. I am still declining. Making money is not what this experience is all about.'

Travis Walton

On 5 November 1975 the twenty-two-year-old Travis Walton was one of a group of seven men who were felling trees on Mogollon Rim, in the

Sitgreaves-Apache National Forest near Snowflake, Arizona. At around 6pm they finished for the day and were driving home in a lorry belonging to the foreman, Mike Rogers, when they noticed a strange light in the trees.

As they rounded a corner they saw a glowing, disc-shaped UFO hovering about 15 feet (4.6m) above the trees. The lorry screeched to a halt and Walton leapt out to investigate while the other men stayed inside. As the intrepid Walton walked towards the UFO it began spinning and emitting an electronic, beeping sound. A beam of light suddenly flashed from it, hitting Walton in the chest and flinging him 10 feet (3m) backwards. His coworkers then sped off in the lorry, leaving him lying unconscious on the ground; it was not until they had seen the UFO lift off and fly away that they plucked up the courage to return. When they did, Walton was nowhere to be seen.

Ninety minutes after the abduction they reported Walton's disappearance to Deputy Sheriff Chuck Ellison. He organised the men into a search party, but three of them refused to go into the woods again that night. 'One of the men was weeping', said Ellison. 'If they were lying they were damned good actors.'

For the next two days they made a detailed search of the forest, but found no sign of Walton. Rumours began to circulate that the loggers – who included Walton's brother, Duane – had murdered the missing man, buried his body in the forest and had then invented the UFO-abduction story to cover their tracks. In order to clear their names the loggers insisted on taking lie-detector tests, which the Navajo County sheriff, Marvin Gillespie, organised on 10 November. The tests were conducted by Cy Gilson, of the Arizona State Office of Public Safety. Although one man was too worked up to enable the test to be declared valid the other five passed. 'I think they did see something they believed was a UFO', said Gilson.

On 11 November Walton's sister received a call from a pay phone. It was her missing brother, who asked her to send someone to fetch him from a nearby petrol station. He was subsequently found lying on the floor of the phone booth in a highly confused state.

When he had calmed down sufficiently he was interviewed with the aid of hypnosis. The first part of his story matched those of his co-workers. He had felt no fear, he said: when the lorry had drawn to a halt he had been excited and had jumped out to run towards the glow. 'Then something hit me', he said. 'It was like an electric blow to my jaw and everything went black . . . When I woke up I thought I was in hospital. I was on a table on my back and as I focused I saw three figures . . . They weren't human.' Walton said that the aliens looked like foetuses. They were about 5 feet (1.5m) tall, with large, hairless heads, huge, oval eyes, small ears and noses, slits instead of mouths and skin as white as mushrooms. They wore tight-fitting, tan-brown robes.

The terrified Walton had grabbed a transparent-plastic tube and had lashed out, but the aliens had scampered away. Then a smiling man – whom Walton took to be a human being – had appeared; he was wearing a helmet shaped like a fishbowl. He had led Walton into a hangar, where a number of smaller, disc-shaped craft were parked. Three other human-looking creatures had met him there and had taken him to another exami-nation table. A mask had been put over his face and he had then blacked out.

'When I woke again I was shaky. I was on the highway', he said. 'It was black, but the trees were all lit up because just a few feet away was the flying saucer.' The UFO climbed up into the sky and this time Walton ran away from it. 'I recognised [that] I was in a village a few miles from my home in Heber', he recounted. 'When I found a phone booth I called my sister.'

Walton thought that he had been gone for only a few hours and could not explain where he had been for the missing five days. He was examined by psychiatrist Dr Gene Rosenbaum, of Durango, Colorado, who con-cluded 'This young man is not lying. There is no collusion involved. He really believes these things'. Walton also took and passed a lie-detector test, which was administered by George J Pfeifer. Leading UFO experts endorsed his claims, while the *National Enquirer* awarded Walton and his co-workers $5,000 for the most impressive UFO story of 1975 (the paper's star prize was $100,000 for concrete evidence of at least one extraterrestrial visitor).

However, the UFO sceptic Philip J Klass was not convinced. He con-ducted an investigation of his own and discovered that Walton, Duane and their mother, Mary Kellett, were avid UFO buffs who frequently reported seeing UFOs. Walton's abduction had also occurred just two weeks after a dramatisation of the abduction of Betty and Barney Hill was aired on US TV.

Klass noted that Mike Rogers and Duane Walton had been interviewed by a UFO investigator while Walton was still missing, during which they had shown no concern for his well-being, even though they claimed to have seen him being zapped by a massive electric shock. They were both convinced that he would return unharmed. Duane even expressed a 'little regret because I have not been able to experience the same thing'.

Duane and his brother, Klass discovered, had regularly discussed making contact with aliens – they had seen enough UFOs to believe that this was a real possibility. They had agreed that one should avoid moving directly underneath a UFO, but decided that the opportunity to climb aboard one would be too great to pass up. They had even made a pact that if one of them was abducted by aliens he would try to persuade them to come back and pick up his brother. Alien abduction was such an ever-present possibility for Travis Walton that he had told his mother shortly before he went missing that if he should ever be abducted she was not to worry: he would return safe and sound. And he was right: although he was groggy when he was discovered, he had no burns from the lightning-bolts with which the aliens had zapped him.

Klass also discovered that before Walton had been polygraph-tested by Pfeifer he had undergone another test with the highly respected Jack McCarthy. He had flunked the first one and McCarthy had accused him of 'gross deception', as well as of resorting to such tricks as holding his breath in order to influence the outcome. McCarthy also suspected that the UFO investigator who had interviewed Walton while under hypnosis had planted some suggestions into his mind. The *National Enquirer*, which had paid for the polygraph test, had persuaded McCarthy to sign a hastily prepared secrecy agreement, but it had been dated wrongly, rendering it legally invalid.

Klass furthermore uncovered the fact that Walton had pleaded guilty to charges of burglary and forgery five years before his abduction. His co-defendant was Charles Rogers, the brother of the loggers' foreman. The Walton family also had a reputation as being practical jokers and hoaxers and Klass even unearthed a possible motivation for such a hoax: the logging crew was behind schedule and Mike Rogers faced paying out on a penalty clause in his contract unless an 'act of God' – which a UFO abduction may have been interpreted as – prevented him and his men from completing the work on time. There was, of course, also the prize money that the *National Enquirer* was offering.

In contrast to Klass, such respected UFO experts as the USAF's Dr Hynek tend to believe Walton. 'It fits a pattern', he told ABC-TV's *'Good Night America'* programme in 1975. 'If this were the only case on record then I would have to say, well, I couldn't possibly believe it. But at the Center for UFO Studies now we have some two dozen similar abduction cases currently being studied. Something is going on.'

Mr and Mrs Barney Hill who believe they were abducted on 19th September, 1961.

The Walton abduction story was made into the film *Fire in the Sky*, starring James Garner. 'If I hadn't believed Travis Walton's story implicitly after talking with him for many hours, I wouldn't have touched the project with a bargepole', Garner said.

'Dissected like frogs'

Shortly after the screening of *'The UFO Incident'* – the made-for-TV movie about the Hills' abduction, which was aired for the first time on 20 October 1975 – a young woman from North Dakota named Sandy Larson reported that she, her boyfriend and her young daughter had been abducted by aliens two months before. They had been 'stripped naked and all parts of our bodies examined'. But the aliens did not stop there: 'Even our heads were opened up and our brains looked at', she said. 'We were dissected like frogs.' Apparently their dissections had no ill after-effects and just a few hours later the three abductees were delivered home as right as rain. They did not even have any scars with which to substantiate the extraordinary tale.

Webbed invaders

The 21-year-old David Stephens was also abducted by aliens just a week after the Hills' movie was aired and described the incident in the July 1976 issue of *Official UFO* magazine. He said that he had been driving in his car with an 18-year-old male friend at the time. Only Stephens had been abducted, however, and his friend had waited for him in the car.

Under hypnosis, Stephens described the aliens as being about 4 feet 6 inches (1.35m) tall. Their heads were shaped like mushrooms, their noses were small and flat and they had no visible mouths or ears. Unusually, they wore flowing, black robes and had white eyes. Stranger still, they possessed webbed hands with only three fingers and a thumb.

Late invaders

Following the abduction of Travis Walton, Air Force Sergeant Charles Moody came forward. He claimed to have been abducted several months earlier, on 13 August 1975. The aliens had spoken perfect English with an American accent, he said, although they did not move their lips. One of them had assured him that 'within three years his people will make themselves known to mankind'. At the time of writing they are more than 20 years overdue – although it must be conceded that they may not necessarily have meant Earth years.

Alien aliens

Steve Harris and Helen White were also abducted from a small town in northern California during the mid-1970s. They recalled the incident while being hypnotised by Dr James A Harder, who was by then working at the Aerial Phenomena Research Organization. Harris said that the alien responsible spoke in English with a slight German, or Danish, accent. He also described the creature, who appeared to be 'human, except that his ears and mouth were slightly smaller and he was fluorescent-looking'. White said that he was 'a blond-headed fellow, with wavy hair and wearing a long kind of thing that looked like a raincoat.'

An alien examination

On the night of 11 June 1976 the 28-year-old Hélène Giuliana, who worked for the mayor of Houston, Texas, as a maid, was coming home from the cinema when her car broke down on the bridge at Romans. She then saw a huge, orange glow in the sky. After it had vanished she found that she was able drive on, but when she got home it was 4am – several hours were unaccounted for. Giuliana's missing time came to the attention of UFO investigators, and under hypnosis she recalled having been carried into a room by small aliens with big eyes. They had strapped her to a table and had examined her, paying particular attention to her lower abdomen.

The influence of The UFO Incident

The stories related above represent just a handful of the alien-abduction reports that were made following the screening of the NBC-TV movie *The UFO Incident*. Indeed, over a hundred were reported during the two years after its airing. There had been only 50 similar reports filed during the previous 30 years; the aliens, some believed, were thus clearly intensifying their activities.

Kidnapping a cop

On 3 December 1967 Patrolman Herbert Schirmer was patrolling the outskirts of Ashland, Nebraska, when an eerie feeling that something was wrong came over him. Seeing a bull charging at a gate, he stopped to make sure that the gate would hold. Later, near Highway 63 – the road that leads to Ithaca and Swedenburg – he noticed a light ahead of him. Believing it to be a truck, he flashed his headlights at it, whereupon the light shot up into the night sky. When he returned to the precinct at the end of his shift he reported seeing a UFO. After he got home he felt ill; a buzzing sound in his ears stopped him from sleeping and there was inexplicable red welt on his neck.

Ufologists are always interested in sightings by reliable witnesses, such as policemen, and Schirmer's case came to the attention of the USAF-sponsored UFO-investigation team at the University of Colorado. Reviewing his report, the team members observed that there were 20 minutes missing from his police log, and in order to find out what had happened during the missing time they suggested that Schirmer undergo regressive hypnosis.

While hypnotised, Schirmer recalled having seen an alien spacecraft coming in to land and its landing gear telescoping from the bottom of the craft. He had tried to drive away, but his police vehicle would not start – either that, or something in his mind was preventing him from driving away. He therefore sat there helplessly while a hatch opened and the aliens got out of the craft. They were between 4 feet 6 inches (1.35m) and 5 feet (1.5m) tall and wore tight-fitting, silver suits. Their hands were covered by gloves, their feet by little, silver boots, while on their heads they wore thin, silver hoods, like an old-fashioned pilot's helmet. Each had a small antenna over its ear. Only their faces were left uncovered, and Schirmer noted that their skin was light grey in colour, their noses were flat, their mouths mere slits and their eyes opened and closed like the shutter of a camera.

As a trained cop, Schirmer instinctively went for his gun, but found that it would not budge from his holster. The aliens then surrounded him. There was a flash, and he passed out. On board the alien ship, the creatures communicated with him in broken English, both vocally and by means of telepathy. They explained that they had been studying human languages.

They told him that their ships were vulnerable to the ionisation caused by radar. They came from a neighbouring galaxy, but had hidden bases on Earth; one was under water, near Florida. They then showed him a film, which incorporated a shot of three alien 'warships' flying against a background of stars that included the Plough. They had come to Earth to study human behaviour, they said. Unfortunately, despite their advanced state, they survived by stealing electricity from overhead power lines, but in such small quantities that the power companies did not notice.

Before he was released, the aliens' leader looked deep into his eyes and implanted the suggestion into his mind that he would not reveal what had happen on board the ship to anyone. Schirmer was next told precisely what to say in his report of the incident. The alien leader also said that they would return and visit him twice more.

Schirmer submitted himself to a polygraph test, which he passed with flying colours. Other psychological tests were carried out and Schirmer was given a clean bill of health. He was regressed again by Dr Leo Sprinkle, a professor of psychology at the University of Wyoming, who discovered more hidden memories. But still the team at the University of Colorado would not accept Schirmer's case as having been a genuine abduction, because although he genuinely believed that he had been taken on board a UFO by aliens, he could present no further corroborating evidence.

The nightly news

One night in the autumn of 1973 Mike Bershad was driving home to Baltimore down Route 40. He had been visiting his girlfriend in the nearby town of Frederick, Maryland. On the road, he had suddenly been overwhelmed by the feeling that he was being watched. He could not remember whether he had seen a light in the sky or whether he had pulled the car over; all he could remember was that he had wished that the car could have gone faster. When he had arrived home it had been much later than he had expected.

Bershad was so disturbed by whatever it was that had happened to him that he sought out the one-time abstract-expressionist artist and full-time ufologist Budd Hopkins, who arranged for Bershad to undergo regressive hypnosis. During the session it was discovered that Bershad had indeed pulled over: he had parked on the hard shoulder and had got out of the car. Some black-clad figures, with chalky, putty-like skin, had then emerged from behind a fence. The aliens had next placed a brass clamp over his left shoulder that had held his head in place; it was connected to a flying saucer. Bershad had then been led up a ramp into the craft, which gave off a quiet, humming sound. He had walked around inside for some time before finding himself lying on a table in a round, white room. He was wearing some kind of nappy. A round, metal bulb, which was extended on an arm from the ceiling, seemed to soothe him. All sorts of blades and other instruments stuck out of it and one of them dug into his back painfully. Then the aliens had pushed a tube into his stomach. Stirrups grabbed his thighs, before lifting and spreading his legs, while an alien examined what was between them.

Hopkins wrote up the story of Bershad's abduction and it made the NBC television channel's nightly news.

A rash of abductions

In 1974, after seeing a TV series about UFOs, a young woman (who is known in the literature of ufology as 'Sara Shaw') approached the UFO investigator Ann Druffel. She reported a strange sighting that had occurred over 20 years before, when she was 21 and staying in a cabin in Tujunga Canyon, California.

On the night of 22 March 1953 Shaw had been woken by a bright light, which she first took to be a motorcycle's headlight. But the light was in the sky, so she looked at the clock to check whether the time was approaching dawn. Shaw was with her 22-year-old friend, 'Jan Whitley'. Whitley got up and went to the wardrobe to get a dressing gown. Shaw looked at the clock again – 20 minutes had passed and Whitley was still standing by the wardrobe. Then Shaw realised that she had read the clock wrongly: two hours and twenty minutes had actually passed. Shaw had initially been kneeling on her pillows while looking out of the window, but now she was sitting on her bed. She had a sense that something strange and terrible had happened.

Druffel arranged for Shaw to undergo regressive hypnosis. Under hypnosis, Shaw remembered looking out of the window and seeing a group of individuals walking through the yard. They entered the house and Whitley fought them while Shaw watched. She recalled being inside a dome-shaped chamber inside an alien craft. Whitley continued to struggle while the aliens tried to take off her pyjama top. The next thing that Shaw remembered was that she was floating above a table, undergoing a physical examination. The aliens used some sort of machine before examining her with their hands. They seemed particularly interested in an old, surgical scar. She also felt that in some mysterious way they had marked her with an 'invisible number four'. The two young women were then floated back to their bedroom. They were told that they would forget everything that had happened to them.

There was one obvious way in which Shaw's story could be corroborated, and UFO investigators accordingly tracked down Whitley. She had not forgotten the abduction: it had come back to her in 1956 in a series of vivid dreams. Curiously, Whitley had another friend, Emily Cronin, who reported an abduction experience that had happened in 1956 that had involved her and Whitley, but not Shaw. They had been travelling in a car together when they had pulled into a lay-by. They had seen a bright light, which then paralysed them. Cronin recalled having been watched by someone through the back window of the car. She had eventually managed to move her finger, which had broken the spell.

Whitley revealed that she had had another, related experience in 1967 or 1968, during which she had been unable to move and had seen the faces of the aliens whom she and Shaw had first encountered in 1953 floating above her. She also reported that she had seen her first UFO during the early 1940s, when she was still in her early teens.

Similar events took place in nearby Panorama City, California, during the 1970s. In 1970, for example, Lori Briggs awoke to find herself paralysed. She then realised that she was not alone in her flat. Furthermore, her nocturnal visitors were not human: they were short creatures, with long, thin hands. While lying on her back, unable to move, she found that she was looking directly into the eyes of an alien.

Five years later Briggs had been awoken in the same way; this time the creatures had told her to come with them. Under hypnotic regression, she recalled having woken to find the aliens standing next to her bed. They had large, hairless, egg-shaped heads – so large that their thin bodies could not have supported them under ordinary circumstances. They had small noses and mouths, but big eyes, which seemed to have bright lights shining from them. When they had asked her to come with them she had not wanted to go, but had found that their will was stronger than hers. The creatures could hover in mid-air, and along with them she had floated through the walls to a dome-shaped craft. She had next found herself inside the alien ship, where there was an examination table which appeared to be made of pink stone. There was a very bright source of light under it, which she had believed to be some sort of X-ray apparatus. She had lain on the table while the aliens examined her. When that was finished, she had said that she wanted to go home and had pressed a button that opened the door. The aliens had courteously said that they would accompany her. Once back in bed, she had found herself paralysed again, but the next morning she had woken with only the memory of being incapacitated and of something staring at her.

However, on this second occasion Briggs had not been alone: she had had a girlfriend named Jo Maine staying with her. Under hypnosis, Maine remembered having seen a bright light and having had the sensation of floating. She was in a tube, she thought, surrounded by light. Then she was lying flat in the dark; some sort of examination was going on. When she was dressed again they had moved on somewhere else, before she had suddenly found herself back in bed, with Briggs lying beside her.

A spaceman in the house

On 17 October 1973 Pat Roach, a divorcée who lived in Lehi, Utah, awoke. She knew that something strange had happened, but had no idea what it was until her two children – Bonnie, aged thirteen, and Debbie, aged six – told her that spacemen had been in the house. Roach did not believe them, of course, and was afraid that a burglar was on the prowl. She therefore called the police, who searched the house and garden and combed the area. They found nothing. However, Roach and her children were too scared to stay in the house alone, so they spent the rest of the night with friends.

Two years went by, but Roach and her children could not forget the incident, which was preying on their minds. So she wrote to the US magazine *Saga*, asking for help and saying that she just wanted to find out what had happened. Her letter mentioned spacemen, so she was put in touch with Dr James A Harder, the noted hypnotist who investigated alien abductions.

Under hypnosis, Roach recalled that two aliens had been standing near her bed when she awoke. They were small, with large heads, pasty, white faces and big eyes. They wore silver uniforms, with a tight-fitting cap or helmet, gloves and a Sam Browne-style belt that carried a small pouch. They had touched her on the arms and had lifted her up. As they had carried her away she had seen her children trying to fight off other aliens in their room. One of them seemed to be a female wearing a maxi skirt, who had long hair which was held back in a headband.

The aliens seemed to have put no great effort into Roach's abduction, and she had apparently floated effortlessly into the waiting craft. She had not really seen the outside of the spaceship, but had merely glided up a stairway and through a hatch. Inside, she had been separated from her children before being stripped and placed on a floating table, where she was given a gynaecological examination. The aliens had showed off some

Although fuzzy, this UFO's unusual shape can be seen.

of their technology to her. Then they had hypnotised her; they had appeared particularly interested in her life story and her emotions. Finally, they had given her clothes back to her and had told her to dress.

Under hypnosis, Bonnie, Roach's older daughter, said that she remembered her mother being examined by aliens. A balding human with greying hair was helping them. She had thought that he was a doctor and said that she had known that he was human because he had 'regular ears'.

Abducting the righteous

Three women – all devout, born-again Christians – were abducted from their car near Stanford, Kentucky, on 6 January 1976. They had been returning from a birthday party to their home town of Liberty when they saw an intense, red glow in the sky to the east. The glow came closer, until it was hovering at tree-top level near the car. All three women saw a domed disc, which flashed three shafts of bluish-white light onto the highway.

The driver, 44-year-old Mary Louise Smith, stopped the car and tried to get out, but the 36-year-old Mona Stafford pulled her back. The lights on the spaceship then went out and the car raced down the road of its own accord. Smith could not slow it down – it was like it was being pulled by an invisible force. An instant later, they were deposited in Houstonville, 8 or 9 miles (12.8 or 14.5km) away. They then realised that they were missing some time and also noticed blistered paint on their automobile and burn marks on their bodies.

All three were regressed by Dr Leo Sprinkle. Smith had a memory block that he could not get past, while the 48-year-old Elaine Thomas only remembered having been observed by short creatures. They were 'like humans, except that they were only about four-and-a-half feet [1.35m] tall and they had fingers that looked like the edges of birds' wings – complete with feathers'. They had put a 'cocoon' around her neck that had choked her and had placed a bullet-shaped object above her left breast.

The regression of the youngest abductee, Stafford, yielded much more information. She remembered having been removed from the car and having been taken into a hot, dark room. Then she had found herself lying on a bed, with her arms clamped. Several small creatures surrounded her; they had grey skin and large, slanting eyes. The rest of their features were obscured by the surgical caps and gowns that they were wearing. A white light seemed to force her back as an 'eye-like' device examined her. Her eyes hurt; her feet were twisted and bent backwards; and she felt something 'blowing up her insides'. (This description would certainly be consistent with a gynaecological examination, but – perhaps because they were modest, Christian women – none of them mentioned this aspect of their abduction.)

All three women insisted on taking lie-detector tests, which were performed by Detective James Young, the senior polygraph operator for Lexington, Kentucky. He said 'It is my opinion that these women actually believe they did experience an encounter'.

Stafford subsequently recovered more memories. She recalled having been taken from one ship to another. She also remembered having been inside a cave or volcano. Later still, she reported another encounter with an alien: a creature dressed in a gold robe had issued telepathic commands to her, which she refused to obey at first. But she had then come to believe that she was under the control of the aliens.

Smith also reported a second encounter. She had woken one night seized with a strange compulsion to drive to Stanford, to the place from which they had been abducted. Once there, she had got out of her car and had stood there for a while, unable to leave. Suddenly, at about 3am, she had run back to her car and had driven off. She had then noticed that three rings were missing from her fingers and later remembered feeling a tugging at her hand while she had stood there waiting.

The Allagash abductions

Jim Weiner, his brother, Jack, and two friends, Charlie Fotz and Chuck Rak, were on a canoeing trip to the Allagash Wilderness Waterway, Maine, on the night of 20 August 1976. Before they went out on to the lake, they built a large fire on the shore to act as a beacon so that they could find their way back to their camp. When they were on the water they saw a light in the sky that was coming towards them. Eventually a spacecraft hovered over them and the light that it beamed out played over the water around them. They observed it for a while before rowing frantically back to shore, where they stood and watched the alien craft fly off. By this time all that remained of the fire was embers; they had no idea how it could have burnt itself out so quickly. Just how long had they been on the water?

After the holiday all of the men had nightmares concerning strange creatures looking at them – they were particularly interested in the men's genital areas. Weiner, who was particularly disturbed by the dreams, met the ufologist and author Raymond Fowler at a symposium, who recognised in Weiner's story the telltale signs of an abduction.

Under hypnosis, Weiner recalled having been taken on board the ship and the aliens examining him. At first he could not remember their faces. (Fowler believed that aliens have special powers with which to induce amnesia.) During a second session of hypnosis Weiner recounted the bedroom visitations and other paranormal events which seemed to follow him around

Fowler interviewed the other men who had been on the trip, too, who also remembered seeing the UFO. Under hypnosis, they recalled having been taken from the canoe. Once inside the ship, they had been stripped. Three of them had sat on a bench while samples of blood, skin and semen were taken from the fourth. The room reminded them of a hospital – cold and sterile. And they all talked about their bodies having been probed with medical instruments. After the examination was finished they had been allowed to dress and were then sent back to their camp. When the alien craft was gone they had been overcome with fatigue. Next morning, they had had little recollection of the event. They did not talk about it – it was almost as if it had never happened.

Strangely enough, none of the men could initially remember the faces of the aliens, but after persistent questioning they finally came up with a description. The aliens were shorter than humans. They had large heads, which were out of proportion to their thin bodies. Their chins were pointed and their eyes large. Their legs and arms were spindly. And their hands had four fingers

6 ❖ Abductions UK

It seems that anything that occurs in the USA happens in Britain three years later. So it was perhaps inevitable that after the USA was hit by an epidemic of alien abductions an extraterrestrial assault on the UK was not far behind.

A secret weapon

Albert Lancashire claimed to have been the first British victim of an alien abduction. It happened in 1942 – during World War II –when he was on guard in a sentry box outside a top-secret radar base at Cresswell, just north of Newbiggin, in Northumbria. He was 27 years old at the time.

First he saw a light over the North Sea and then a strange cloud rolled in; he initially thought that he was being attacked by some new, German, secret weapon. As he stepped out of the sentry box to investigate he was hit by a beam of yellow light and felt the sensation of floating. The next thing that he knew was that he was waking up in a confused state and was lying on the ground.

He forgot about the incident until around 1963, when UFOs became all the rage, and he began to get the feeling that he had been in one. In October 1967 there was wave of UFO sightings in Britain and at around that time he also read of the Hills' abduction. This prompted a series of strange dreams in which he awoke in a strange room to find an oriental woman lying on a bed; he was given a pair of goggles and a man dressed in white was also there.

Swimming with the dolphins

In January 1981 Linda Taylor, who was in her late twenties, was travelling home by car from Southport to Chorlton, in Manchester. At around 7.30pm she was driving around the East Lancs Road, which was usually quiet, when a huge light appeared in the sky. It appeared to be keeping pace with her car, which jerked about and then slowed right down.

An old car of a peculiar model that Taylor did not recognise then appeared in front of her. It was dangerously close, so she took her eyes off the light for a minute. When she looked back, the light had turned into a huge flying saucer that hovered over an area stretching roughly from Leigh to Worsley. The old car had mysteriously vanished from the road. Taylor pulled into a petrol station and pointed out the UFO to a man who was filling his car (the man was never traced). At that point the UFO tilted sideways and shot off skywards.

When Taylor reached home she felt unwell and furthermore discovered that her coat was missing; two hours of her time also seemed to be unaccounted for. She underwent hypnosis, but recovered no memories. However, she had a recurring dream following the incident. In it, she was in a room with a blond-haired, blue-eyed man wearing a white suit who took her to visit a dolphin, which he said was sick; Taylor was supposed to touch it and make it well again.

After her encounter Taylor became a UFO investigator.

A rejected abductee

Many are called, but few are chosen – or so the Bible says. When it comes to UFO abductions, however, it seems that many are called and many are chosen. However, one who was definitely not chosen was the then 77-year-old Alfred Burtoo, who, on 12 August 1983, was fishing on the banks of the Basingstoke Canal, near the army barracks in Aldershot. At around 1.15am Burtoo noticed a bright light land some way down the towpath. Two figures then approached him and Burtoo's dog growled warningly. The figures were aliens, about 4 feet (1.2m) tall and dressed in pale-green overalls and helmets. They beckoned to him and he obediently followed them.

They led him down the towpath to a spacecraft, whose shape was similar to a spinning top. He climbed a ladder and entered it. Once inside, a voice told him to stand under an amber light. Then he was asked his age, to which he responded truthfully. 'You are too old and infirm for our purposes', the voice said. 'You may go.' So Burtoo clambered back down the steps and returned to his fishing. When he looked back he saw the UFO start to glow; it hummed like a generator and then sped off into the sky.

Burtoo died in 1986, but stuck to his story to the end.

The photofit abductor

On 1 December 1987 Philip Spencer, a former police officer, was walking across Ilkley Moor, in Yorkshire, to visit his father-in-law, who lived in a village on the other side of the moor. It was a 5-mile (8-km) journey and he had left the town of Ilkley at around 7.10am. A keen amateur photographer, he had his camera with him, intending to take some pictures of the town from the top of the moor. He also carried a compass in case he got lost.

Near an overgrown quarry he heard a low, humming sound. At first he thought that it came from a low-flying aircraft, but then a small, green creature approached him. It immediately scuttled away while Spencer shouted at it. As it stopped and turned he took photograph of it before giving chase. On rounding an outcrop he saw a huge, silver UFO, which consisted of two flying saucers that were connected together. The UFO was the source of the humming, which now increased in intensity. Suddenly it shot skywards and disappeared into the clouds.

The dazed and confused Spencer retraced his steps to Ilkley, which was, to his surprise, bustling. Although he thought that it could not be any later than 8.15am the town-hall clock said that it was 10am. Fearing that he was losing his mind, Spencer now realised that his camera contained proof of his sanity. He therefore travelled to nearby Keighley, where he knew that there was a one-hour photo-processing service. The wait was agonising, and when he was finally given the pictures he immediately tore open the package that contained them. The quality of the photograph was poor, but the image was unmistakable: it showed a green creature with large ears, short legs and long, thin arms – in short, the alien that he had seen that morning.

Spencer was now in a quandary. He was trying to rejoin the police force and the last thing that he needed was for it to become generally known that he had seen an alien – the force would be sure to doubt his mental health or would possibly brand him a hoaxer. But because he was now convinced that he had indeed come into contact with an alien he wanted to know more. And he also wanted to discover what had happened during the 'missing time'.

He therefore contacted the Manchester UFO Research Association under a false name, using a post-office box as his address. When he eventually met the investigators he was happy to hand over his photograph , as well as the negative, for testing. They quickly concluded that the negative had not been tampered with, that the picture was not a photograph of a photograph and that no photographic trickery been used. The photo was genuine.

Spencer also noted that his compass had been useless since the encounter, and the investigators found that its polarity had been reversed. In order to for this to have been done this a pulsed, magnetic field must have been used; without the help of rare and expensive equipment the process of producing such a field is dangerous and possibly even lethal – assuming that you know how to do it in the first place.

Six weeks after the encounter Spencer was visited by men from the Ministry of Defence who wanted to take the picture away, but it was with the investigators at the time. He also began to have dreams in which he was lost amid a starry sky, and he started to wonder if the dreams had anything to do with his missing two hours. He consequently agreed to undergo hypnotic regression.

Under hypnosis, he revealed that he had been abducted. He recalled that when he had first seen the alien creature he had become paralysed. Then he had felt himself levitating and floating over the quarry. When he had seen the UFO a door had opened in its side. Then everything had gone black.

When he awoke, it was in a brilliantly lit room. He was told not to be afraid: they were not going to harm him. Then he was placed on an operating table and a beam of light was passed over him. He closed his eyes and then felt something uncomfortable in his nose. Next, he was given a guided tour of the ship. On looking through a porthole he could see the stars; below him lay the Earth, and he realised that he was in space. After that he was shown a couple of films. One was full of apocalyptic images, but he would not reveal what the other one was about.

Afterwards, he had woken up in the same spot from which he had been abducted. He had spotted the alien walking away from him and it was then that he had shouted out, the alien had turned and he had taken the picture of it. Although the picture was blurred, under hypnosis Spencer gave a clear description of the alien, which matched the image. He also said that the aliens were about 4 feet (1.2m) tall, with big eyes and pointed ears. Their arms were long and their hands enormous, with fingers like sausages. They had two toes on their feet, in a funny, V-shaped arrangement.

Curiously enough, it was not the first time that little green men had been seen in the area: it had happened less than 500 yards (457m) from where Spencer had encountered his alien, at the White Wells Spa. In 1815, when the caretaker was opening up the bathhouse there, he had put his door key into the lock; the key, he said, had then revolved of its own accord. Inside, he had been shocked to see that the bath was already occupied by 'a lot of little creatures dressed in green'; the creatures had then taken off their green garments in order to wash. On seeing him, they had all run off. The caretaker had been paralysed with fear and had not chased after them.

After the investigation Spencer was re-employed by the police force on the strength of character references from former colleagues, which said that he was honest and trustworthy. He had certainly had no reason to lie about what he had seen on Ilkley Moor – indeed, by telling the truth he had risked losing any chance of resuming his career with the police.

Lost in Dorset

In September 1990 James and Pamela Millen went camping in Dorset. One night they woke up at around 3am. James noticed that there were a number of orange balls of light dancing above the next field and called Pamela to point them out to her. The couple found them hypnotic, but James managed to tear himself away to get his camera. Neither of them is very clear

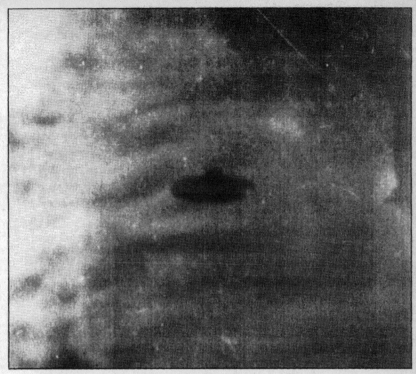

The disk shape described in many sightings can be seen in this photograph.

about what happened next. When James returned he thought that he had been away for just a couple of minutes, but there was now a pile of cigarette butts at Pamela's feet. When they looked at their watches it was 5.40am: some two-and-a-half hours had gone missing.

A vague recollection of what had happened during that missing time returned later, however. James recalled lying on his back on something cold in a white, circular room and being attended to by a man in white robes. He did not know what the man was doing to him, but believed that it was something beneficial.

Another near miss

Elsie Oakensen, the head of a teachers' centre in Daventry, encountered a UFO on her way home on 22 November 1978. It had been a disturbing day: at lunchtime she had felt an odd, tightening sensation around her head. On setting off on the 6-mile (9.7-km) journey at 5.15pm she found that one of her sidelights was not working and she therefore had to drive with her headlights dipped.

When she reached the traffic lights at Weedon she turned right, on to the A5 towards Towcester. She noticed two bright navigation lights – one red, one green – ahead, in the sky above the road. At first she thought that a low-flying aircraft was going to crash on to her, but then she realised that the lights were stationary. As she drove underneath them she saw that they marked the ends of a huge, grey, dumb-bell-shaped craft. It was hovering soundlessly above the point where she would turn off the road to follow the lane to her home, in the village of Church Stowe. (Although this huge spacecraft was hovering above a busy main road at around 5.30pm no one else reported having seen it.)

Oakensen watched the craft in fascination as she climbed the hill into Church Stowe. Suddenly her car's engine cut out and the headlights failed. Bright lights flashed at her from above; the beams were so brilliant that she could see nothing in the darkness apart from them. When she turned the ignition and touched the accelerator pedal the car started again as if it had never stopped, but when she arrived home it was 5.45pm. The journey – which she covered twice at day and which usually took her 30 minutes – had taken 45 minutes. (On the following day she timed the trip just to make sure how long it took and discovered that some 15 minutes had indeed gone missing on the night in question.) When she reached home she discovered that her sidelights were working again; they did not malfunction after that. Later that evening Oakensen again felt a tightening sensation around her head.

Although no one else had seen the craft hovering above the A5 there had been another UFO sighting that night. Four young women who were driving in a car 4 miles (6.4km) from Church Stowe had seen two streaks of light flash across the sky. Then they had noticed a red and a green light some way to the south that seemed to be keeping apace with the car. The car's engine had begun to lose power, but the two lights had next vanished incredibly quickly. The engine had returned to normal and the car had functioned perfectly well after that.

Oakensen subsequently underwent hypnosis and while hypnotised remembered again feeling the tightening sensation around her head when her car's engine had cut out. The pain had been intense and she had become hotter and hotter. Then two figures had appeared; they looked grey against the glow. Oakensen came to believe that she had been visited by aliens, who had scanned her. She somehow felt that she had been promised a return visit, but had ultimately been rejected. (Like Alfred Burtoo, she may have been too old.)

Oakensen later became deeply involved in the UFO-related movement. She joined a witness support group whose member counselled each other; together they experienced a growing spiritual awareness. She also became interested in psychic phenomena, corn circles, ley lines, pendulums, crystals and natural healing. She wrote poetry and practised as a medium. She furthermore published a book, *One Step Beyond . . . A Personal UFO-abduction Experience*, all of which goes to show how much a chance encounter with an alien being can change a person's life.

Alien assassins?

On 11 June 1980 a man was found dead in a coal yard in the West Yorkshire mill town of Todmorden. The body was that of 56-year-old Zigmund Adamski, a one-time Polish prisoner of war who had managed to escape from captivity had settled in England after the war. He had worked as a miner for 30 years and had recently not a been well man, but during the months before his death he had been on leave and the rest had done him the power of good.

At 3.30pm on 6 June 1980 he had left his home in Tingley, near Wakefield, to go to the shops. A neighbour saw him in the street and asked him if he was going for a drink; Adamski replied that it was too early. He was not seen alive again.

Adamski's body turned up five days later – almost to the minute – twenty-five miles (40km) away. Nobody knew what had happened to him in the meantime. Nobody knew how he had come to be in the coal yard either. His body was discovered by Trevor Parker, the owner's son, at 3.45pm. It was lying in a hollow at the top of a pile of coal, near Todmorden railway station and within view of the line. Parker was adamant that it had not been there at 8.15am, when he had been at the same spot, and the coal yard had been locked during the intervening hours.

There were other mysterious aspects to the case, too. The time of death was estimated to be anywhere between 11.15am and 1.15pm on the day of the body's discovery, which meant that it had been lying in full view for at least two-and-a-half hours of daylight – that is, unless it had been put there after Adamski had died. There was no obvious cause of death; there were a few, minor, external wounds, but none of them would have been fatal.

Parker had noticed a large, brown burn on Adamski's neck and the pathologist concluded that he had been burnt with a corrosive substance. Yet this would not have killed him either, and besides, the burn had occurred two days before he died, according to the pathologist. And where had he been for the five days since he had gone missing? He had certainly not been sleeping rough. Indeed, he had been well taken care of: he had only one day's growth of beard on his chin, although his stomach was empty, suggesting that he had not eaten on the day of his death. The police were baffled.

However, the publicity surrounding Adamski's death was enough to attract ufologists, although Zigmund Adamski was no relation of the first alleged modern alien-abductee, George Adamski (the name is quite common in their native Poland). But there had been a wave of UFO activity over the Pennines during the late 1970s and ufologists were on the alert. Although some suggested that Adamski had been abducted and then dropped onto the coal heap from above, no one could discover any evidence with which to take the case further forward.

Alan Godfrey, one of the policemen who had first been called to the coal yard, was not looking for an extraterrestrial explanation – he was a sceptic who took no interest in UFOs. A down-to-earth Yorkshireman, he would have laughed if a friend had told him that he had seen one. At around 5.05am on 29 November 1980 he was looking for an elusive herd of cows that had been reported running loose in a housing estate. He had already made several unsuccessful attempts to find the cows earlier in his shift, but decided to give it one last try before he finished work at 6am. He accordingly set off in his panda car up Burnley Road, which runs out of the town in a north-westerly direction. He had travelled only a few hundred yards when he saw a very bright light ahead. It could not have been the early morning bus because he had already seen that pass; something about it attracted him to it.

He drove to within about 100 feet (30.5m) of the light and then stopped, amazed. What he saw appeared to be a giant, fluorescent top in the middle of the road. There was a line of five dark windows about two-thirds of the way up. The domed, upper part of the craft was still, while the bottom was spinning in an anti-clockwise direction, making the nearby bushes and trees shake. Godfrey calmly observed the craft. The beam of his headlights was reflected from its surface, so he assumed that it was made out of metal. He tried to use the police radio to call for assistance, but neither the UHF nor the VHF channel worked. Although he later admitted that he was too terrified to get out of his car, he felt perfectly safe inside and picked up his clipboard and sketched the object on the back of a traffic-accident report. By comparing its size to the width of the road and the height of the street lamps he jotted down his assessment of its dimensions, estimating that it was 20 feet (6m) across and 14 feet (4.m) high. The windows were oblong, 3 feet by 1 foot (91cm by 30cm), and the entire thing was hovering 5 feet (1.5m) above the surface of the road. Suddenly, without a sound having been made, Godfrey found himself 100 yards (91m) further down the road. The UFO was gone.

He initially reported that he had turned his car around and had driven directly to the police station. But six weeks later he recalled that he had first got out of the car and looked upwards, into the sky, to see if the UFO had really gone.

Godfrey then picked up a colleague from the police station and together they went back to place where he had seen the UFO in order to examine the scene. There they found that there was nothing that he could have mistaken for a UFO. Furthermore, the only remaining evidence of the UFO were dry, swirling-shaped patches on the road over which the UFO had hovered; the rest of the road was uniformly wet, as a result of the rain that had fallen earlier that night.

Back at the station, Godfrey's colleagues began teasing him and he decided not to make an official report of the incident. However, he became increasingly convinced that what he had seen had been real. Later that day he had one of his first flashback memories: he suddenly recalled that just before the object had disappeared he had heard a voice in his head saying 'You should not be seeing this. This is not for your eyes'.

When Godfrey turned up for work the next night he discovered that an anonymous man had reported seeing a UFO answering the same general description as the one that Godfrey had observed hovering around the area that night. Godfrey then decided to file a report, only to find that three other policemen, who had been searching the moors for stolen motorbikes, had seen a similar UFO just twenty minutes before him. After they had radioed in their report of the sighting they had seen the UFO again, this time travelling in the direction of Todmorden. Even though they were convinced that it was not a helicopter or plane, they checked with Leeds/Bradford Airport, which, however, could offer no instant solution to the UFO's identity. A special constable also reported a UFO sighting made at around that time.

All of this corroborating evidence helped Godfrey to reassure himself that he had not gone mad. He now noticed that his foot had been injured and that his sturdy, new boots had been damaged: the left one looked as if it had been dragged over a hard surface, but he could not recall any such incident. He also remembered that it had not been damaged before 29 November.

With the aid of UFO investigators Godfrey subsequently painstakingly reconstructed the events of the early morning of 29 November and discovered that 15 minutes could not be accounted for. The missing time left him totally flummoxed; he wanted an explanation for what had happened and eight months later agreed to undergo regressive hypnosis.

Under hypnosis, he again remembered getting out of the car, but then recalled having seen a light appearing under the UFO. He had got back into the car, but when he had attempted to drive off it would not move. Then, in middle of the session, the regressed Godfrey cried out and covered his eyes; he was connected to an electrocardiogram (ECG) machine, which showed that his heart beat was rocketing upwards at this point. The hypnotist, the psychiatrist Dr Joseph Jaffe, had to go to great lengths in order to calm him down.

Eventually continuing the session, Godfrey remembered that he had been blinded by the light when he had felt something take hold of him – he was being carried, floating. Suddenly he was in a room. There was a table in it, as well as a man wearing white sheet and a skull cap. He was about 6 feet (1.83m) tall, with a beard and a long, thin nose. Somehow Godfrey knew that his name was Joseph. There were eight small, metallic figures in the room, as well. They were about 3 feet 6 inches (1.6m) tall, with heads 'like a lamp' and eyes resembling single, vertical lines. Godfrey squirmed when they touched him, but Joseph told him telepathically not to be afraid: the robots were his. Furthermore, there was a big, black dog in the corner.

Joseph led Godfrey to the table. A bright light was shining and Godfrey recalled receiving the telepathic message 'This is not for your eyes'. Telepathically again, he was told to get onto the table. He experienced a pain in his head, which Joseph soothed. The robots removed his left boot and examined his foot. Then bracelets were put onto his right wrist and left ankle before being plugged into some type of machine. He smelt a sickly odour and saw flashing lights – similar sensations to those that many people experience when undergoing a general anaesthetic. Details of his past life flashed before him and his mind was probed by a series of questions. He got the impression that Joseph was telling him that they had met somewhere before and he suddenly had a very vivid childhood memory of seeing a huge ball of light in his bedroom.

Godfrey remembered little of his sessions of hypnosis; the tapes of the sessions were played back to him afterwards and he was at a loss to explain them. Jaffe could not suggest any reason why Godfrey would have made up what he was saying and concluded that something very strange had happened to him.

Although PC Godfrey never claimed to have been an abductee his experience changed his life: West Yorkshire Police declared that he was mentally unfit for duty and sacked him. 'I know what I saw on the road that night. It was real', he said. 'As for what I said under hypnosis, I just don't know. It seemed real, but it might have been a dream.' But why would anyone dream of being abducted? As in the case of Zigmund Adamski, the mystery remains unsolved.

All in the family

In 1988 the 45-year-old Carol Thomas and her 24-year-old daughter, Helen, were working in a Birmingham mill. Each morning Helen went round to her mother's house and together they made the 15-minute walk down a number of alleyways to the mill.

As they walked to the mill on the morning of 30 March 1988 it was still dark. They heard a distant, humming sound and suddenly a bright searchlight shone down on them from above. It was directly above their heads and appeared to be becoming bigger and bigger. The next thing that they knew was that they were stumbling dizzily down an alleyway. By the time that they reached the mill they discovered that they were late for work – even though they had left Carol's house at the same time as usual.

They reported suffering from a curious type of what appeared to be sunburn after the incident – the skin on their arms and faces was blistered and red. They also experienced discharge from their navels, as well as nosebleeds.

Under hypnosis, Carol recalled how the light – which had first been above them – had appeared below them. She saw the moon and seemed to be travelling towards it. Then she found herself in a white room, which had windows all around it. Naked, she was strapped to a table and a wet cloth was spread over her legs. She was surrounded by little aliens with big, black eyes and three long fingers on each hand. They were led by a taller alien, which had blond hair and blue eyes and was wearing a silver suit with a badge on it. The aliens pushed a long, thin, glass tube through her navel; she thought that they were taking eggs from her ovaries. An odd-looking cup was put onto her head and she was shown a series of shapes on a screen and then a war film. After that she had found herself back in the alleyway again.

Carol said that Helen had been with her on the ship and that she had begged the aliens not to harm her daughter. Helen confirmed this under hypnosis. She, too, had found herself lying naked on a table, her legs having been covered with a wet cloth, next to her mother. She had cried. Helen had seen the little aliens, although she thought that they only had two fingers. What she took to be a camera was hovering over her. The aliens had pushed a thin rod up her nose and had implanted a small, silver ball into it. A wire was fed into her ear and a thin, glass tube into her navel. She also reported that two wires were inserted in her cervix; something was removed from her body, she believed.

Helen seems to have been given a more comprehensive physical examination than her mother. As with Carol, they had placed a metal cap on her head and had showed her images on a screen. She also remembered seeing her mother with a tall, blonde alien wearing a silver suit. The alien, she said, looked like a beautiful woman. The touch of the aliens, both women reported, was damp. Indeed, everything inside the ship seemed clammy. Helen recalled observing an alien feeling the texture of her leather coat. Back in the alleyway, her mother had asked why her coat was wet. Neither of them could remember why.

However, Helen's hypnosis revealed something even more interesting: she recalled having been abducted before, when she was five. She had been taken from a field full of buttercups before having been examined in a room by what she took to be weird-looking children. They had given her a strange stone, which Carol remembered her having when she was a child and which she had kept under her bed. Helen also began to remember numerous other occasions on which she had been abducted. Indeed, it seemed that aliens had been plaguing her for all of her adult life.

Working in the woods

At 8pm one night in September 1996 Mary and Jane – two young mothers in their thirties living in Scotland – went out to buy some coffee in a nearby village. They took Peter, Mary's 10-year-old son with them; Jane's 14-year-old daughter, Susan, stayed at home watching television.

While driving on a remote stretch of road they saw two bright lights. In the sky above them was a huge, dark shape. They stopped and got out of the car for a better look. The UFO was 80 feet (24m) across and shaped like a triangle, with a red light at each corner. It then sped off across the sky at incredible speed. After they had bought the coffee they were returning down the same road when they saw the UFO again: this time it was hovering over the car, as if it was observing them. They were frightened, but then it shot off towards the horizon again.

When they reached home Mary called the UFO Research Association's hot line, which advised them to go back to the spot where they had seen the UFO and to take a camera and binoculars with them. They did not have either, but went back anyway. This time Susan came along, too.

There was no sign of the UFO when they got back to the place where they had originally seen it, but they became aware of a weird glow in a nearby field; through the gloom they saw a number of small creatures milling about. Terrified, they drove to Jane's home. Her brother was there and lent them a pair of binoculars to take with them before they again returned to the scene. Hiding behind a dry-stone wall, they observed the aliens carrying objects – which they took to be cocoons – from a small wood. The aliens seemed to be approaching, so the group fled again.

Jane subsequently began to get the impression that she had been taken aboard the UFO and had been examined – the examination had not hurt, but had instead made her feel happy. A few weeks later the other three also began to recover memories of having been on the ship. UFO investigators went to the sight of the alleged abduction and found burn marks on the ground. They ascertained that a heavy object had certainly rested on the ground, although there was no road access to the site. The surrounding trees and bushes were furthermore covered in a strange, cobweb-like substance.

Alcoholic aliens?

In July 1995 Steve and Annie asked their neighbours, Mike and Debbie, to their Derbyshire home for a barbecue. At around 11pm that night a flying saucer descended on to the garden; they spotted it when it was about 20 feet (6m) above their heads. A door at the bottom of the spacecraft opened and bathed the garden with light. They then fell into a trance and later remembered only the light dimming to a pinpoint as the craft moved away,

UFO at night.

leaving them feeling nauseous and dizzy. The whole episode, they thought, had lasted a matter of minutes, but when Steve looked at his watch it was almost midnight.

They called the police, who took statements from them. Curiously, two of the four glasses of cider that had been on the table when they had spotted the UFO had disappeared and were never found again. Their physical reactions continued for the next few days and they found it hard to sleep. In an attempt to deal with the aftermath of the encounter they agreed to undergo regressive hypnosis.

Under hypnosis, Debbie recalled having suddenly found herself alone in a room, unable to move her arms or legs. She was surrounded by aliens with enormous, black eyes. They were doing something to her, hurting her. She became so distressed by her recollections that the hypnosis session had to be terminated.

Annie, too, remembered seeing big, black eyes, but they had belonged to a creature with a pale face and a pointed chin that had appeared in the garden. Another two had then materialised and had pulled her towards the illuminated door of the craft. Inside were more of the little creatures, which only had three fingers. They had dragged her towards a table and had started taking off her clothes. She recalled them examining her and doing something to her navel.

Under hypnosis, Steve similarly remembered having seen small aliens with large, black eyes. He seemed to have been restrained within a transparent tube. He had seen a map of the solar system and had noted that the aliens seemed to be carrying balls of white material in their hands. He got the impression that at one point he had been in a second, larger, ship.

For his part, Mike was too traumatised to risk hypnotising him. All four were profoundly affected by what had happened to them, even though they had not believed in UFOs or alien abductions before the incident occurred.

A girls' night out

On Thursday 16 July 1981 three young women had enjoyed their weekly night out at Tiffany's, in Shrewsbury. They left Tiffany's at 2am for the 20-minute drive back to their homes in Telford New Town. The 27-year-old Viv Hayward was driving; next to her in the front seat was the 20-year-old Rosemary Hawkings, a mother of three; and in the back was the 26-year-old Valerie Walters.

Their route took them down the A5, through the village of Atcham. While driving on the road to Norton their collective mood suddenly changed and all conversation ceased. Later they reported that they thought that this was part of a 'conditioning process'. Across the fields they saw some lights – two white, two red. Hawkings wound down the window in order to take a better look and saw that the lights were attached to some sort of object. They did not know what it was, but were not unduly concerned until it started to follow them. Walters peered out of the back window and noticed that craft had windows along its sides, while the lights on the base seemed to be tilting towards the car.

It was then 2.10am. They were just ten minutes from home so Hayward put her foot down, but the engine did not respond and began to splutter. The car was losing power and the three women began to panic: the last thing that they wanted was their car to break down on a deserted road in the early hours of the morning in the presence of a UFO. Suddenly, however, the spacecraft disappeared into the clouds. The car's engine regained power and they sped on down the road, convinced that they had just had a close encounter with an unidentified flying object. Racing on to Telford New Town, they went straight to Malinslee Police Station to report the sighting. The women said that they got there at 2.55am, but the police report stated that they had arrived at 2.40am. If the police report was true, they had lost around 20 minutes.

Under hypnosis, Hayward recalled that everything had gone very quiet when the engine failed. Then she had had the feeling that she was floating. The car seemed to have been lifted from the road, which had disappeared under a white cloud. She recalled having been alone in the car while it was lifted vertically into the UFO, through two big doors that had opened in the underside.

Small, hairless aliens, with big eyes and wearing green cloaks, had taken her out of the car and had placed her in a reclining chair similar to a dentists' before holding her down. The aliens were very strong, she said. They had wanted to discover things from her, particularly 'how humans are made'. They had told her not to be afraid, but she felt that they were taking something from her body – it was as if they had put their hands inside her legs and were pulling on her bones. This hurt terribly and she cried out in pain, but their only response was again to tell her not to be afraid. They had then given her body a thorough examination and had scanned it with a 'big light', a procedure which had left her paralysed so that she had had to be carried back to the car. The next thing that she remembered was driving along the road again, with the UFO gone.

When regressed, Hawkings reported a similar tale. She, too, said that everything had gone quiet and that she had had the sensation of floating (but she had not been in the car, a statement which corroborated Hayward's recollection). She had found herself alone in a room which had a table in it and had been very frightened. She had no idea what she was doing there, but had a strange compulsion to get onto the table; it was something that she had seen in a film, she said, and it calmed her. Then a number of robots 4 feet (1.2m) tall – 'round on top with a round body and round leg' (like R2-D2 in the film *Star Wars*) had entered. Hawkings said that they had not given her a full medical examination – 'they just wanted to have a look'. She had the impression that she was in an area leading off a larger room waiting for her friends.

However, under hypnosis, Walters told a slightly different story. The UFO, she said, had come at them. Its lights were blinding and she had felt dizzy. She remembered having been in the car with Hayward, although Hawkings had gone – mysteriously having been 'beamed out' of the car. She recalled that the car had then come to a halt; the doors were open, so she had got out to look for Hayward. Next she remembered having floated into a room. Two aliens had entered – one male, one female. They were different from the aliens that Hayward had seen, however, being 6 feet (1.8m) tall, with white skin, blue eyes and long, dark hair, but like Hayward's aliens they were wearing long, green cloaks.

The aliens seemed inordinately interested in fashion. While Walters was told that the women had been abducted for purposes of observation, Hayward was given a full medical and Hawking's reactions were being studied, it was Walters' clothes that they had been especially interested in. The female alien had even slipped her high-heeled shoes off Walters' feet and had then tried them on; she had had difficulty walking in them, though.

Walters was the only one who had questioned the aliens – not that it had got her very far, however. She had asked them who they were, but they had curtly replied that she was not to know and that she would not understand. Walters later came to believe that her encounter with the aliens had not been as benign as she had first recalled: they had done something to her, she thought, that was 'gynaecological in nature'.

7 ❖ Abductions world-wide

Alien abduction is a world-wide phenomenon, although different types of alien appear in different parts of the world. But because people are becoming more familiar with the language of alien abductions their stories tend to coincide.

A Canadian abduction
In what would later become Canada's most notorious alien-abduction case on record, the 14-year-old David Seewaldt revealed under clinical hypnosis what it was like to be seized by an alien spacecraft and then closely examined by repulsive-looking creatures.

The event that he described happened in Calgary, Alberta, on 19 November 1967. At around 5.45pm on that fateful Friday Seewaldt had just left a friend's house and was walking the two blocks home. It was late autumn and darkness had fallen. He took a short cut across a field; normally the walk took just a couple of minutes. Suddenly he heard a high-pitched sound. He turned round to see a silver-grey object flying in the sky. Dotted around the centre of the UFO were coloured lights that were flashing on and off.

The next thing that he knew he was running up to his front door, with the sinister craft still hovering overhead. He burst into the house and ran upstairs. His older sister, Angela, followed him and found him cowering behind his bed in a state of blind panic. 'What happened?', she asked, grabbing him, 'Why are you home so late?' It was 6.30pm by then; 45 minutes had passed since he had left his friend's house. 'I . . . I was chased by a flying saucer', said the clearly terrified boy. He managed to describe the spacecraft and to give a detailed account of its pursuit. But the ordeal that he described would have lasted only a minute or so and there was no way that he could account for the missing time.

Seewaldt was usually a calm and mild-mannered child, but he was a bundle of nerves for the rest of that weekend. His worried parents called the celebrated ufologist William K Allan, who hosted a UFO-related show on the local radio station, CFCN-AM, in Calgary. Allan had a meeting with the boy, but could coax no more information out of him.

Seewaldt gradually forgot about the incident and the household settled back into its regular routine. Then, in April 1968, five months after the incident, Seewaldt awoke one night having had a nightmare. He had dreamt that he had been taken aboard the alien spacecraft and had been given a medical examination by creatures so repulsive that he could only describe them as 'monsters'. He was convinced that his dream was an accurate recollection of what had happened during the missing 45 minutes.

The nightmare had left the boy badly shaken and the Seewaldts again turned to Allan for help. Allan realised that he would have to use regressive hypnosis in order to get to the bottom of Seewaldt's tale. He therefore secured the services of a local dentist who used hypnosis in his practice, but when the dentist hypnotised Seewaldt it transpired that he had been so traumatised that he had mental block. When he was asked what had happened after he had first seen the craft he was unable to speak; his legs shook violently and he began to perspire.

Under the supervision of a psychologist at the University of Calgary, Seewaldt was subsequently videotaped while under hypnosis. In order to try to get through the mental block it was suggested to him that he recount what had happened as if he were seeing it unfold on television. This is the tale that Seewaldt then recounted.

After he had first seen the spacecraft he had turned and run. Then an orange beam had emerged from the bottom of the ship. When it reached him he had fallen into a trance, after which the beam had seized hold of him and had lifted him into the ship. Once inside, he had seen two monsters, which had brown, scaly skin, like a crocodile's, holes for their noses and ears and slits for their mouths. They were about 6 feet (1.8m) tall, with four fingers on their hands and feet and no thumbs.

Four of them had put him onto a cot and had then started to examine him. They had stripped him of his clothes, including his underwear, which had upset him greatly. They had lifted up his head and had examined his hair, eyes and nose. One of them was talking to the others in a language like none that he had ever heard; he described it as a sort of buzzing, like the sound that emanates from a beehive or a high-voltage, electrical spark. After they had let him put his clothes back on again, the aliens had taken him down a hallway to another room, in which there were all sorts of bright lights. They had laid him on a table. Then came what he described as being the most terrifying part of the ordeal: a grey blanket was thrown over him before a huge, orange light descended and was shone on to him; one of the monsters next took a grey needle and stuck it into his arm.

The next thing that he knew was that he was walking through a computer room before emerging into a hallway. The orange beam had then reappeared and Seewaldt had next found himself back on Earth. A high-pitched whine was coming from the spacecraft as he dashed for home; just as he arrived the spacecraft shot upwards and disappeared.

Not fade away

The multiple abductions of a Canadian rock musician named Jack were reported in *Flying Saucer Review* in 1984. He first recalled having been abducted at the age of two, when he was taken from his pushchair by aliens with big, black eyes. He had been put onto a table inside a room and felt that his thoughts were being siphoned from his head. The aliens had told him that this was a test: they wanted to know if he was suitable for their purpose (although he did not recall what the purpose was). When he was six he was abducted again, this time along with his father. Jack's father subsequently underwent regressive hypnosis and recalled the abduction as well. Then, at the age of ten, he and his friend, Jim Voss, were taken from Twelve Mile Creek, near their homes.

By the time that he was 16 Jack had joined a rock-and-roll band. On the night of 16 October 1971 the band was returning from a party at around 1.30am when strange lights appeared on the road ahead. They thought that there had been a road accident until their van skidded out of control. It finally stopped at the side of the road, whereupon a small alien ordered them to get out. Some members of the band refused and there was a struggle, during which a drum was kicked out of the van before rolling across the road. The alien asked – telepathically – what this odd instrument was.

The alien explained that they wanted to test the young men, but only had enough facilities for three; volunteers should therefore step forward for testing. Jack, the drummer and the bass-player stepped forward and were taken aboard the UFO. Jack recalled that they were in some sort of drugged, or hypnotic, state.

The bass-player, Calvin, was taken into a separate room. Sam, the drummer, and Jack were told to take off their clothes. They complied before lying down and being inspected with lights and instruments. Blood and hair samples were taken. The two young men asked some questions, including where the aliens came from. They replied 'A long way away . . . if we told you you would not understand'.

Before the band members were released Jack gave their abductors one of their records, which he was carrying in his bag, as a gesture of goodwill. To this day Jack believes that the inhabitants of some planet in a distant galaxy are grooving away to Canadian rock music.

European encounters of the fourth kind

On 1 November 1954 an Italian woman named Rosa Lotti was walking through a wood on the way to Cennina when she came across a weird, egg-shaped craft. Two 3 foot (91cm) tall aliens then grabbed her. She did not have a very clear recollection of the incident, but remembered that she had been paralysed by a beam of light and that the aliens had been talking in what sounded to her to be Chinese. She did not remember whether she had been medically examined, but during the encounter she lost a stocking and a bunch of flowers that she had picked. Some village boys had come to her rescue, who saw both the spaceship and the aliens.

In September 1955 the 27-year-old Josef Wanderka was riding his moped down a road in Austria when he inadvertently rode straight up the ramp of a flying saucer. He apologised profusely to the occupants, who explained – in perfect German, naturally – that they were from the 'top point of Cassiopea'. Even though they were plainly adept at interstellar travel, they were fascinated by his moped and wanted to know how the engine worked. The aliens were of the 'Nordic' type: tall, with blue eyes and blond hair. Fearing that they might be harbouring totalitarian tendencies (Austria had been de-Nazified relatively recently), he launched into an anti-fascist diatribe. They evidently found this so boring that they kicked him out of their flying saucer without subjecting him to an invasive medical examination.

In July 1965 the 41-year-old Maurice Masse was tending the crops on his farm near Valensole, in France, when he heard a strange, whistling sound. An egg-shaped craft then descended from the sky and landed nearby. At first Masse thought that it was a new helicopter that the French Air Force was trying out, but then a number of what appeared to be small boys got out. On closer inspection they turned out not to be boys at all: they had big, pumpkin-shaped heads, thin mouths and big eyes – classic greys. Masse would have left it at that had the aliens not begun picking his lavender. He tried to remonstrate with them, but was zapped by a beam of light. It was subsequently suggested that Masse had made up the last part of his story and that he had actually been taken on board the spacecraft. He later admitted that he had not told the whole story because something had happened that he found too embarrassing to talk about. He particularly did not want his wife to know about it (so perhaps it is not just Brazilian men that aliens abduct for the purposes of sex).

In July 1968 a 25-year-old man was approached by some tall aliens with domed heads and huge, oriental-shaped eyes on the Grodner Pass in the Dolomites. They had small robot with them. They communicated telepathically with him and passed on some useful information, including that they came from a 'far galaxy' and that 'everything is God, man'. More pertinently, they told him that the Earth's poles were about to shift, that its crust would crack and that humankind was about encounter a lot of trouble.

A 31-year-old Belgian businessman had a narrow escape on the evening of 7 January 1974, when he was travelling down a deserted border road near Warneton. He was trying out his new radio-cassette recorder when the car's electrics suddenly packed up. When the car had finally cruised to a halt he got out, intending to replace a fuse. Then, in the road in front of him, he saw a domed craft. Two aliens got out of it; they were about 4 feet 6 inches (1.35m) tall, with pear-shaped heads, big eyes, narrow mouths, small noses and long arms. As they approached him one pulled out a tube-shaped instrument and pointed it at him, whereupon he heard a painfully high-pitched whistle and felt a shock at the base of his skull. At that moment another car drove down the road, causing the aliens to run back to their ship and speed off. The driver of the second car saw the flying saucer take off; he then stopped and ran over to help the businessman, who was still temporarily paralysed. The second driver, who lived nearby, next went to find some friends to help him to search the area. 'If I come up with nothing', he said, 'I will keep quiet. Without proof, no one would believe a word of this.'

On 5 February 1978 in Soria, Spain, a 30-year-old vet named Julio was driving in his car with his dog, a pointer named Mus, in the early hours of the morning. He did not remember what had happened to him during the drive, but his eyes later hurt and he seemed to have lost some time. Under hypnosis, he recalled having been suddenly blinded by a light. Then he had been led into a room and a soothing voice had reassured him that they only wanted to borrow his dog for examination. But the frightened dog had lost control of its bladder – with unpleasant consequences. The aliens had then decided that if the dog was going to behave in that way they may as well experiment on the human instead, and had accordingly taken samples of Julio's semen, blood and gastric juices. The aliens had told him that our sun hurt their eyes, which was why they usually only appeared at night. Their world was a dark and polluted place, they had said, but humanity's was a beautiful jewel and a rare oasis of fertility in an otherwise sterile universe. That is what had brought them to Earth, they had explained: they wanted to study the humans' world before they destroyed it, just as the aliens had destroyed their own. But Julio was warned to be careful because not all of the aliens who came to Earth were so benign: there was a bunch of ugly little brutes, for instance, which was intent on reprogramming human beings biologically. After that Julio had blacked out and had next found himself back in his car, where he had sat in a daze for a long time.

On 2 April 1980, in the early hours of the morning, Aino Ivanoff was driving her car near Pudasjarvi, in Finland. Suddenly a mist came down.

The next thing that she remembered was that she was in a room, lying on a table being examined by small aliens. They seemed rather worried and told her that war was bad and that she should join the peace movement. Then they explained why they were so concerned about the fate of humankind – they could not have their own children (which explains a lot).

Hairy giants

On the night of 6 December 1978 Fortunato Zanfretta, a 26-year-old security guard in Genoa, Italy, saw four lights moving about in the courtyard of a deserted house in the Marzano district. He tried to call his headquarters to report the intruders, but his two-way radio failed. He could not fetch help either, as his car's electrics would not work. So he therefore went to investigate himself.

As he walked up to the front gate the lights in the courtyard moved towards him, before disappearing around the back of the house. Emboldened, Zanfretta followed them and stuck his head around the corner at the back of the house. He was suddenly pushed to the ground and caught a glimpse of his assailant, who quickly vanished. Zanfretta scrambled to his

UFO flying over New Mexico on 16th October 1957. There has been no explanation given for this object.

feet; as he ran back to his car he heard a loud, whistling sound behind him, followed by a blast of heat. He called for help on the radio, which was now working. It was then midnight, much later than when he had arrived at the house. After that he blacked out, and an hour later his friends found him in a field. Nearby they discovered a horseshoe-shaped depression about 24 feet (7.3m) wide.

Under hypnotic regression, Zanfretta recalled having seen a triangular spacecraft. He had been abducted by aliens who were 10 feet (3m) tall and covered with green hair. Their ears were pointed and they had two narrow, triangular-shaped eyes that sloped upwards; in the middle of their foreheads, among the folds of skin, was a third, more human-shaped, eye. The hairy giants had taken him into a circular room, where they had put something onto his head that had caused him a great deal of pain.

The strange case of 'Dr X'

The 'Dr-X' case is one of the most famous French alleged alien abductions on record. Although the abduction itself did not last long, its recollection did not rely on regressive hypnosis and there was also a large amount of evidence supporting it.

'Dr X' was a well-known and respected biologist. He allowed the French ufologist Aimé Michel to publish an account of his abduction provided that Michel did not use his name – hence his pseudonym, 'Dr X'.

In 1968 the 38-year-old Dr X was living with his wife and 14-month-old son in a house that overlooked a valley in south-eastern France. On the night of 2 November 1968 he awoke to hear the cries of his son; there was also a thunderstorm raging outside. His wife was sound asleep, so Dr X got up to attend to the child. He did so with some difficulty because a couple of days before he had been chopping wood and had slipped; the axe had struck his left leg, puncturing an artery and causing extensive internal bleeding. The wound had been treated by a doctor, who had examined it again on the previous afternoon. He already had problems with his right leg. During the Algerian War a mine had exploded and had fractured his skull. This injury had damaged the left hemisphere of his brain, as a result paralysing the right side of his body. Although the paralysis had passed after a couple of months the muscles on his right side were left permanently wasted. His disability had cost him his career as a musician and he still could not stand on his right leg properly.

Despite his walking difficulties, he managed to totter into his son's room. The boy was standing up in his cot shouting 'rho, rho' (this was the word that the child used to describe a fire burning in the hearth or, indeed, any bright light). He was pointing to the window and Dr X assumed that he was indicating the lightning flashes that were visible through the cracks in the shutters. He got the boy some water and settled him down. While he was doing this he could hear a shutter on a window in an upstairs room blowing back and forth in the breeze. Half asleep, he went up and closed it, noticing as he did so that the room was bathed in a pulsating light.

After closing the shutter Dr X felt thirsty and therefore went downstairs for a glass of water. Still puzzled by the intermittent light, he went out on to the terrace to investigate it. It was 3.55am by the kitchen clock, he noted. Once outside, he immediately saw the source of the light: it was being emitted by two silver, disc-shaped UFOs that hovered over the valley. They had long antennae sprouting from them, which seemed to be collecting electricity from the storm clouds. The furthest end of the antenna would begin to glow, the light would build up along its length and would then suddenly be discharged onto the ground in the form of a lightning bolt. The build-up happened rhythmically and the emission illuminated the whole valley with a flashing light.

The two craft then merged into one and the pulsating light ceased. After that the unified object moved up the valley towards him. Dr X noticed its underside, which was covered with dark, rotating bands, causing patterns that defied the laws of science and logic. When the craft got within 500 yards (457m) of Dr X he had the feeling that it had noticed him. It then turned a bright beam of light onto him, bathing the whole house in an intense glow. He raised his hands to protect his eyes, but suddenly there was a loud bang and the craft shot skywards, so fast that it looked like a single streak of light.

It was 4.05am when Dr X went back inside, which surprised him as he did not think that he had been outside for one minute, let alone ten. He returned upstairs, woke his wife and told her what had happened. As he talked excitedly to her he paced up and down, stopping every so often in order to make notes and draw sketches of what he had seen. His wife suddenly observed that he was walking normally. He pulled up his left pyjama leg and saw that the axe wound had healed completely, which would normally have been impossible in such a short period of time. What was more, his withered right leg was now functioning perfectly, too.

Eventually Dr X went back to bed. Later on that night his wife was disturbed by him talking in his sleep. She noted down what he was saying; one of the things that he repeated was 'Contact will be re-established by falling downstairs on 2 November'. When he awoke at 2pm the next day she did not tell him about this, but suggested that he write to their friend, the ufologist Aimé Michel. Dr X asked why he should do so, whereupon his wife discovered that he had no recollection of his UFO sighting on the previous night. And when she showed him the notes and sketches that he had made he became alarmed.

Later that afternoon Dr X tripped and fell down the stairs; it was as if something had grabbed his leg, he said. He hit his head during the fall and suddenly memories of his experiences of the previous night flooded back to him. Twelve days afterwards he dreamt about seeing another UFO. It was not like the ones that he had observed before, being bright, luminous and triangular. Three days after that he felt an itching sensation on his stomach and on the following day a red triangle appeared around his navel. The dermatologist was baffled and wanted to write a scientific paper about it, but Dr X prevented him from doing so.

Dr X then contacted his friend, Michel, who discovered that there had been a rash of UFO sightings around the area where Dr X lived on the same night that he had seen his flying saucers. Michel suggested that the red triangle might be psychosomatic in origin. Dr X agreed, only to find that a similar red mark then appeared on his son's stomach the next day.

The experience left Dr X feeling depressed and confused. He gradually began to take an interest in ecology. The triangle disappeared, but later reappeared occasionally; other injuries that he sustained healed miraculously. But his house seemed to be constantly plagued by poltergeists and aliens, who would take him on journeys over impossible distances.

A good communist is kidnapped

Alien abductions even happened in the former Soviet Union. A good communist named Anatoly was walking along the shores of Lake Pyrogovskoye in May 1978 when he was grabbed by two aliens who wore dark suits made out of Cellophane. They took him for a spin in their spacecraft, but it appears that they really just wanted a chat.

He asked them to help the Soviet Union to fight the evils of the world – that is, capitalism, which Anatoly believed caused world-wide poverty. Although they acknowledged that helping the poor was a noble aim, the aliens found the idea impractical: 'If we helped the poor,' they argued, 'then we would have to help the not so poor, then we would end up helping everyone'. They gave him a drink which tasted like lemonade laced with salt. If their civilisation was so advanced, he asked, why did they not drink vodka? 'Perhaps if we drank vodka we would not be such an advanced civilisation', the aliens astutely replied.

The aliens then kindly dropped him off by the lake. When he got home and revealed what had happened to his wife, she told him to keep quiet about seeing aliens in case he found himself doing hard labour in a gulag. However, Anatoly felt that by not reporting the abduction he had not fulfilled his duty to the state and therefore told the local commissar about it. The commissar believed that Anatoly was fabricating the story in order to avoid a court martial. Nevertheless, the proper procedures had to be followed and Anatoly was examined by a psychologist, given a lie-detector test and put under hypnosis. They could find no evidence that he was making it up – in fact, when he described events more fully his story even became convincing. And as he had tried to recruit the aliens to the communist cause they let him off.

Brazil nuts?

Per capita, there have been more UFO sightings in Brazil than in any country apart from the USA. Furthermore, as we have already seen, alien abductions practically began there.

Ten years after Antônio Villas-Boas was abducted for sexual purposes in 1957, another abductee wrote to a leading Brazilian weekly magazine in response to a piece that it had published called 'I Saw a Flying Saucer'. The anonymous letter purported to come from a leading citizen of the city of Fortaleza, the capital of the province of Ceara. He had withheld his name, he explained, because of his prominent position: if he disclosed his identity people would think that it was either a publicity stunt or that he was a lunatic or liar. He also said that he had been with four other people at the time in question. Two of them were well-known doctors, another was a local bank manager and the fourth was a metallurgical engineer from São Paulo, who spent his holidays in Ceara.

All five were keen fishermen, and in June 1967 they had spent a weekend fishing in the beach resort of Morro Branco, in the municipality of Cascavel, not far from Fortaleza. They were out fishing at around 3am on a Sunday morning. There was a full moon, but the sky was cloudy and dark.

Suddenly they heard a low, humming sound, so low that it became painful to the ears. Then it stopped as abruptly as it had begun.

The engineer went off to investigate the source of the noise while the rest went on fishing. Five or six minutes later they heard the humming again, only this time it was louder and more intense. It appeared to be coming from a hill around 500 yards (457m) behind them, and when they turned around they saw pulsating beams of smoky-coloured light spreading across the sky. Frightened, they frantically started to pack up their gear, but then the engineer suddenly appeared behind them and told them to stop. Gesticulating with a gun in his hand, he ordered them to climb up the hill, towards the lights. The others thought that he was joking and laughed – that is, until he fired a bullet and said that he would kill them all if they did not do what he said. His eyes looked strange and they decided to obey him, thinking that he had gone insane.

They accordingly staggered up the hill at gunpoint. The lights had now disappeared, but they heard weird sounds in the darkness. The engineer responded by shouting 'We're coming'. Then he urged on his fishing companions, who, by this time, were all suffering from splitting headaches. At the top of the hill they saw a huge UFO hovering 30 feet (9.1m) above the ground; it was 15 feet (4.6m) tall, round, finned and glowed in a phosphorescent-green hue. The top was covered with funnels (from which the beams of light had come) and there was ramp leading up to a square hatch which they climbed, into the UFO.

They found themselves in a room that was about 6 feet (1.8m) tall and had no windows or doors. The light that illuminated it was soft and gentle on their eyes. A strange-looking grille was situated in one corner, near the ceiling. That was all that there was to see. They were very frightened, but a voice told them to be calm: nothing would happen to them, it said; they had only been summoned to answer some questions. The voice explained that their answers would have important implications for the universe in general, and then went on to say that it had come from very far away, but could not explain from where because they would not be able to understand.

The first question that it asked was how they had been made (it did not know what a woman was). It also wanted to discover what humans were made of, what they ate, how many people lived together on the planet and what it was called. Did they live with other species and, if so, did the species also talk on 'frequencies'? The alien was interested in what the men had been doing when they were abducted. Fishing turned out to be a concept that it could not grasp, no matter how clearly the fishermen tried to explain it. The alien furthermore wanted to know whether humans had travelled to other planets, whether they lived on them and also whether they lived under the Earth's crust. When he asked how long a human life span was the men had to explain what a day, a month and a year were. The alien laughed when he computed just how short a human life was.

The abductees found it very stuffy in the windowless room and plucked up the courage to point out to the alien that they would die if they did not get some air. Miraculously, a triangular window appeared in the smooth, seamless walls and a light breeze blew into the room. The alien then considerately asked if there was anything else that they needed. One of the doctors replied that they needed an explanation for their abduction and the others said that they would not answer another question until they were told what was going on. The alien retorted that there was no point in concurring since they would not be able to understand, but it finally conceded that it would answer their questions. They then fired so many at it that it had to stop and ask them to talk one at a time.

The alien explained that it and its five companions would not make themselves visible to the men as they were very different from humans, although made of similar substances. Their life span was 300 years. It said that they had come from Goi to study Tonk, which is what they called the Earth. This was their first visit, but aliens from other planets had visited Earth before. The humming sound that the craft made was used to attract humans and lights had been used to hypnotise the engineer. The alien was interested to know what the engineer was carrying in his hand. After they had explained what a gun was the alien realised that this was how four of his companions had been killed. He said that it had been their own fault, however, because they had been following 'something that flew in the air'.

The alien revealed that there were other inhabited planets nearby, but that those who lived on them were much more advanced than the people of Earth. Aliens would be living among humans within a year, it predicted; creatures from Goi already dwelt on Earth, but in places to which humans never went and, indeed, where they would not be able to live – indicating the polar icecaps. The alien also said that two people from Earth lived on Goi; they had travelled there many years previously and had now forgotten about the Earth. Before the alien went, it said that it needed some of their things – one item from each man. 'We heard nothing more', said the letter, 'and woke up.'

The five men then found themselves back on the beach. It was 5.20am; two hours and twenty minutes had elapsed, but they had no subjective idea of how much time had passed. Puzzled, they trekked back to the hill, but although they could see the footprints that they had made when they had ascended it there were none to show that they had come down. None of them had any recollection of how they had returned to the beach. They climbed the hill and found a shallow crater at the top which seemed to have been caused by a blast of air. Back on the beach they found that some of their possessions were missing – one item from each man.

The letter concluded with the writer making the following statement: 'The purpose of writing this narrative is solely that it should be used as data for research purposes'.

Alien *Doppelgänger*

A prominent Brazilian industrialist reported a similar incident to the fishermen's. It had happened when he was 18. At 7.30pm on 28 February 1974 he had been at home when he had suddenly found himself elsewhere: in a square room – with no windows or doors – the colour of smoked glass.

'Keep calm, we are your friends', said a voice, which came from a box with flickering lights on it in the corner; it appeared to be a tape recorder or a translation device of some sort. A door mysteriously opened in the wall and an egg-shaped machine appeared. An intense, yellow light shone down on him from the ceiling before an exact replica of himself stepped out of the machine. His *doppelgänger* patted him on the back and said, in a voice identical to his own, 'Keep calm and wish me a good journey, for I do not intend to harm anyone'. He then stepped though the wall.

At that exact moment a large screen appeared in the room, which showed images of the replicant in the abductee's home. However, there were some significant differences between the abductee and his *Doppelgänger*. The abductee was affectionate by nature, for instance, but saw the *doppelgänger* treat his younger sister very tersely, which surprised and upset her. Indeed, he was rough and thoughtless with everyone around him. Even though he was only 18, the abductee was already working for the family firm and watched as the replicant went out on business in his place. It became clear that he did not know anything about money, or even how to write.

The screen prompted the abductee to help his *Doppelgänger*. Watching the screen, the abductee saw himself hovering above the replicant and whispering advice. At other times he could see through the replicant's eyes. On one occasion, however, the screen was switched off: this was when the replicant had left the apartment at night. It was switched on again when he returned in the morning. The screen was also switched off when the replicant visited a rainforest (he seemed particularly concerned about the welfare of plants and trees). The abductee furthermore watched as the alien took numerous photographs of Rio de Janeiro, although he noted that the camera that he used was not the abductee's own.

All this time the young businessman was able to talk to his abductors via the box in the corner. He asked them what they wanted with him. 'We need to conclude some tests', they replied. They assured him that he would not be harmed: they were friendly and only wished to help, they said, but added that 'the less you say about this, the better'.

They said that they could not tell him who they were, but revealed that the world from which they came was very different from Earth. They wanted his help. He asked why he should assist them if they were invading Earth, whereupon they protested that they were not invaders but had come for the benefit of the human race. A good Catholic, he asked whether they knew about God; everyone did, they responded. And he also asked what the thing that had replaced him was. 'He is an image that can be touched', they said. 'Inside him there is one of ourselves and a recording of your mind.'

The abductee said that he was held for 24 hours and that he never once felt hungry, thirsty or tired during that time. In the room was a stool for him to sit on and a bed that was fixed to the wall, with a shelf beside it. When the screen went blank the abductee expressed a wish to have something to read – photographic images of a newspaper, books and a *Spider Man* magazine then appeared on it. (He later discovered that the issue of *Spider Man* that he had read in the room was not yet available on the news stands.) For his part, the replicant took a lot of his books on Brazilian history, geography and science. He also helped himself to newspapers, flowers, leaves, photographs and a card, as well as promotional material from the family firm.

The young businessman's watch had stopped during his abduction, but started again when he was returned, exactly 24 hours later. When he tried to explain to his family that he had been abducted and then replaced by a *doppelgänger* they not unsurprisingly found it hard to believe, although they conceded that he had been acting strangely for the past day and could offer no alternative explanation for his behaviour. What is more, one of the family-firm's employees said that he had seen him walk through a wall, although he had felt like flesh and blood to the touch.

Guided by the light

In 1972 the leading Brazilian ufologist Irene Granchi was contracted by an army general – who had also trained as a doctor – who claimed to have been abducted by a UFO.

The incident had happened in March 1969. On the night in question he had been out for a meal at Barra da Tijuca, an isolated spot. After dining on shrimps and beer, the general – who was alone in his car – set off for home at around 2am. As he drove along a section of dirt track the engine suddenly cut out and the car trundled to a halt near a place called Morro do Chapeu ('Hat Hill' in English). He got out and inspected the engine, but could find nothing wrong. The road was deserted and by 2.45am he had given up all hope of getting help. It was at that point that he saw a light approaching him around the hill. At first he thought that it was a lorry, but

Flying UFO in New Mexico. This picture was taken by a student who was photographing the area for a geology project.

then he realised that the light was brighter than anything that he had seen before. As it came closer he noticed that it was hovering about 1 foot (30cm) above the ground.

He walked towards it as if in a trance, following it for 300 or 400 yards (274 or 366m); the ground felt unusually smooth and he appeared to be treading on 'solid light'. When he reached the source of the light he saw it was a spacecraft which had a translucent wall about 10 feet (3m) square, with metal attachments at the side. The wall then tipped up, just like a garage door. Inside, he saw chamber, whose far end seemed rounded.

There were already three people in the chamber: an engineer, a woman who was a law graduate and a doctor. The doctor – who appeared to be very much at home – told them that they had been brought there to see something that they had never seen before. He also said that they were in no danger and that he would be grateful if their response was peaceful.

The rounded end of the chamber then turned into a screen and he noted that they appeared to be travelling across the landscape at an amazingly fast speed. Next, the city of São Paulo hove into view and they seemed to hover above it at a height of about 100 feet (30m). Before he knew it, they were above another large, Brazilian city, which he did not recognise, but thought that the others did. The spaceship then moved on again at an apparently incredible rate until they reached Rio de Janeiro. Afterwards, the doctor asked them whether they had enjoyed what they had seen. He then said 'This will be useful to you, to each in his own way'. (What the general himself gained from the experience was a sensation that time was not as linear as he had once thought.)

After the doctor had said goodbye the general left the chamber and crossed the 'solid light' to his car, which now worked. He drove a mile down the road and then stopped at a bar to attempt to make sense of what he had seen; he ordered a coffee and tried to convince himself that he had had a hallucination. Then he went home and slept.

Over the next few months he studied the available literature on UFOs and tried to evaluate his experience. He was sure that he had been awake throughout and that he had not been dreaming. Using his medical experience, he concluded that he had not been hallucinating: the experience had been unique and isolated and there was nothing that he could identify that would have induced it. His own behaviour at the time had been stable, while routine medical tests could reveal no physical problems. He wanted to unravel the philosophical and intellectual implications of his abduction and also reported the case in order to furnish others with scientific data. However, he balked at undergoing hypnosis.

An alien hitchhiker

Onilson Pattero was abducted not just once, but twice. On the first occasion, on 22 May 1977, he was driving home to Catanduva from São José do Rio Preto in his blue Opala. He was 41, married with two children and worked as a library administrator in the state of São Paulo.

At around 2.55am he crossed the Tiete river and the Anhanduva Falls. Soon afterwards he saw a hitchhiker at a petrol station and stopped to pick him up. The young man had short, fair hair and deep, penetrating, blue eyes. He said that his name was Alex. He mentioned that he was 'not from here' and was carrying a silvery object that appeared to be a cigarette case, although he said that he did not smoke. It was still 25 miles (40km) to Catanduva and Pattero stopped for a coffee; Alex had only a sip of mineral water. He said that he was on his way to Itajobi, which lay a few miles beyond Catanduva, to find a job. Pattero offered to drive him there, but Alex did not want to be taken all the way to the village and jumped out of the car in a deserted spot.

After Pattero had turned around to drive back to Catanduva the radio in the car packed up; then the engine spluttered and died. Suddenly a circle of blue light moved slowly across the car. It seemed to make everything transparent, and as it passed over the dashboard Pattero could see the engine beyond it. He initially thought that it was a strange optical illusion caused by the moonlight before realising that it was overcast and raining and that there was, in fact, no moonlight. A larger circle of bright, blue light then shone down the road at him. He feared that it might be an oncoming lorry and tried to move the car on to the hard shoulder, also flashing the car's lights to signal its presence. The light only grew brighter, however, and he lowered his head onto the steering wheel to try to protect his eyes.

When he heard no vehicle approaching he looked up and saw a UFO hovering about 30 feet (9m) above the road, some 15 yards (14m) away. For a moment he thought that it might be a helicopter, but soon realised that this was no helicopter, but a flying saucer. It looked, he said, like two metal soup plates that had been welded together rim to rim. The object itself was dull, with no noticeable features; it was around 20 feet (6m) high by 30 feet (9m) wide. There was a halo of light around it, but he could locate no specific source for this.

It had grown hot and airless inside the car, so Pattero got out; it was intensely hot outside, too. He then noticed a tube extending from the bottom of the craft towards him and tried to make a run for it. He had got less than 40 yards (37m) before he felt what he thought was a lasso ensnaring him. He turned around, but could see nothing holding him. After that he saw the beam of blue light running over the car, rendering it transparent. He had not yet finished paying for the vehicle and was worried that he would face financial difficulties if it were damaged. Then he fainted.

About an hour later two young men from Itajobi were driving past when they saw an unconscious Pattero lying face down on the road; next to him was his car, with the driver's door flung open and the headlights on. They immediately went to call the police. When the police arrived they found a road map of northern Brazil lying open beside the car. Inside, Pattero's suitcase had been opened and ransacked, which surprised Pattero after he had come round because he had locked the suitcase and the key was still in his pocket. The map had been inside the car. Nothing was missing and the vehicle worked perfectly.

Pattero was taken to hospital, where he was passed fit. Strangely enough, however, his hair had turned jet black, but after a few days it returned to its normal, chestnut colour. He developed an itching feeling around his abdominal region and blue spots appeared on his hips and buttocks, which turned yellow and then disappeared. No cause could be found for these physical symptoms and he was in perfect health otherwise. Regressive hypnosis later revealed that he had been abducted.

Nearly a year after his first abduction, on 26 April 1978 Pattero was travelling home at night again when his car's engine cut out and a beam of light passed over him that appeared to make his car transparent.

On this occasion he was subsequently taken into a spaceship, through what he described as a sort of 'curtain'. Inside was Alex, the erstwhile hitchhiker, who told Pattero not to be afraid. He was shown a fabulous laboratory and Alex then told him to take off his clothes. There followed a detailed physical examination by what seemed to be humans, who did not say a word. After that his hands and feet were secured with steel rings and he was put into a long case. While this was happening he saw three 'men' walking by – one of them was an exact replica of himself and he was dressed in the same clothes that Pattero had been wearing when he was first abducted.

He remembered nothing else until he awoke on the top of a hill; it was reputed to be a spooky spot, where neither cattle nor men dared venture. Pattero shouted for help; fortunately a gaucho heard him and his boss, the ranch-owner, came to his rescue. Pattero then discovered that it was 3am on 2 May. He had been missing for seven days, but was still clean-shaven. He was also over 500 miles (805km) from home, in a different state. His car had been found – with the driver's door wide open – not far from home and his family had practically given up hope of ever hearing from him again.

Eminent ufologists later endorsed his case and he was regressed again. However, there were some inconsistencies in his story. After giving a series of interviews to the newspapers he then told a reporter that the authorities had forbidden him to speak to the press. He was subsequently denounced at a UFO conference by the ufologists who had originally supported his story on the grounds that he had claimed that he had not watched the TV series 'The Invaders', although his wife revealed that he had. This omission made him an unreliable witness.

Abducted from a rooftop

In 1979 Zenon Carlos Rios wrote to a Brazilian magazine to report that he had been abducted by aliens, an experience that had taken place six years earlier, when he was eighteen.

After a row with his older sister he had been thrown out of the family home. The house had a flat roof and he decided to stay up there until things had cooled off. The only reason that anyone ever went up to it was to check the water tank or the television aerial and he reasoned that if he hid there he could slip down into the house and steal food from the fridge when everyone was out.

That night he fell asleep next to the cistern. He was woken by a whooshing sound, like that made by a rocket. He looked up to see an egg-shaped craft, about the size of a small car, hovering about 6 feet 5 inches (2m) above him. Its near side consisted of one huge window and through it he could see two humanoids sitting at the controls. Their faces were calm and peaceful, but this did not reassure him – indeed, Rios was paralysed by the sight of the spacecraft and feared that it would hit him. As it edged nearer to him a door opened and he was sucked into the craft by a blast of air. Once inside, he was overwhelmed by the smell of gas and fell into unconsciousness.

When he woke up he was back on the roof, with the sun beating down on his face. His body ached, especially his head and back. He noticed that he was lying in a different position from that in which he had fallen asleep. He thought that it was about 10.30am, but when he looked at the clock on the wall of the bus station he saw that it was 12.30pm. He made his way downstairs in considerable pain, to discover that he had been missing for a week. His family had assumed that he had gone to stay with relatives in Bom Sucesso. Rios asked whether anyone had gone up onto the roof in the meantime and ascertained that one of his brothers had indeed done so: on the night on which Rios had disappeared their television pictures had been distorted by interference and so he had gone up to fix the aerial.

Hundreds of miles from home

On 4 January 1975 the 28-year-old Carlos Diaz was returning home from his place of work in Bahía Blanca, Argentina. When he got off the bus, just 100 yards (91m) from his home, a powerful beam of light shone down on him from the sky and he found that he could not move. The air around him then began buzzing quietly, whereupon a gust of wind lifted him off his feet. He guessed that he was about 8 feet (2.4m) above the ground when he lost consciousness.

When he came round he found himself inside a plastic sphere around 10 feet (3m) in diameter. He tried to move, but his body was paralysed. There were small holes in the plastic which allowed him to breathe and he discovered that if he turned away from them he felt ill. The sphere seemed to be travelling at a rate of knots.

After about 15 minutes three aliens approached him from behind. They were humanoid, about 5 feet (1.5m) tall and moved very slowly. Their skin was greenish and felt like a rubber sponge. They were naked and had no mouth, nose, ears or hair of any sort; instead of hands they had suckers on the ends of their arms. One of the aliens grabbed him, while another attempted to pull out his hair. Diaz tried to struggle, but they were very strong and he eventually passed out.

Some time later he was awoken by a man, who took him to hospital. There he discovered that he was in Buenos Aires, more than 200 miles (321km) from his home. Numerous doctors interviewed him and the military authorities wanted to know what had happened to him, too. It did not seem possible for him to have travelled by conventional means from Bahía Blanca to Buenos Aires in the time available. Some researchers claimed that a paper that he had bought in Bahía Blanca bore his story out, but others said that his tale was riddled with discrepancies.

Hopping continents

In May 1968 Dr Gerardo Vidal and his wife were driving the 100 miles (161km) from Chascomus – 80 miles (129km) away from Buenos Aires – to Maipu, in the south of Argentina. They were following another couple, but somehow their friends lost sight of them. Although they waited for them when they got to Maipu, the Vidals never arrived.

Two days later they had a phone call from the Argentinian consulate in Mexico City asking them to collect the Vidals from the airport and warning them that Mrs Vidal was ill and would have to be hospitalised. On his return to Argentina Dr Vidal explained that while they had been driving along the road to Maipu they had suddenly found themselves surrounded by a dense fog that seemed to have appeared from nowhere. The next thing that they knew was that they were sitting in their car on some unknown side road, suffering from terrible headaches and a general feeling of fatigue. When they asked passers-by where they were they were shocked to discover that they were in Mexico – over 4,000 miles (6,437km) from Buenos Aires.

Abductions that failed

On 28 November 1954 Gustave Gonzales and José Ponce were driving to Petare, about 20 minutes away from their home in Caracas, Venezuela. Suddenly they saw a glowing, spherical object, about 10 feet (3m) across, blocking the road in front of them. They stopped the car and got out to investigate, whereupon a small, hairy alien approached them. Gonzales grabbed it, but the creature fought back. While the two of them were struggling Ponce ran to the nearest police station, which was only a couple of streets away. As he ran he saw two more of the aliens, who had apparently been collecting rock and soil samples. On seeing him they fled to the sphere and jumped into it.

The creature that was attacking Gonzales now unsheathed its claws. In response, Gonzales pulled out a knife and stabbed it. The knife hit the alien on the back, but the blade just bounced off, as if the creature was made of metal. Another alien then stepped from the sphere to give his companion some assistance and shot a beam of light at Gonzales, which left him temporarily blinded. The two aliens then jumped aboard the craft, whereupon it blasted off into the skies. Gonzales took to his heels and sprinted to the police station, where he and Ponce were accused of being drunk. However, a subsequent examination of Gonzales revealed claw marks on his back.

Furthermore, a few days later a doctor came forward and said that he had seen Gonzales fighting with the alien, but had not wanted to become involved.

Two weeks later the hairy aliens again tried to abduct some humans. This time their intended abductees were Lorenzo Flores and Jesus Gomez. Both aged 19, they had been out hunting on the night of 10 December 1954 and were on their way home, travelling down the trans-Andean highway in Venezuela, when they stopped for a rest. A flying saucer then landed near them and four aliens got out of it. They were only about 3 feet (91cm) tall and were covered with hair.

They seized Gomez and tried to drag him aboard their craft, but the youth was not eager to comply. Flores grabbed his rifle and hit one of the aliens with it. 'It felt like I had hit a rock', said Lorenzo. 'My gun broke.' Gomez, who had been screaming, now fainted. Flores rushed to his assistance and was so concerned about his friend's welfare that he did not see what had happened to the aliens (who had presumably thought better of it and had fled back to their ship). Gomez and Flores then made their way to the local police station, where they reported the incident. When they were examined they were found to be covered in scratches, as if they had been attacked by animals.

However, it seemed that the hairy aliens had not given up, for six days later another Venezuelan named Jesus was grabbed by a hairy alien after he had slipped off the road to relieve himself in the parkland near San Carlos. Again a friend came to the rescue and took Jesus to hospital in a state of severe shock.

After 1954 all the small aliens who appeared on Earth seemed to have moulted. And why hairy dwarf aliens only appeared in Venezuela has not yet been explained.

Gaining time

Missing time, it seems, can work both ways – it does in Chile, at least. On the night of 25 April 1977 Armando Valdes, a corporal in the Chilean Army, was on exercise on a desert plateau 12,000 feet (3,658m) above the town of Putre, in Arica province. At around 3.50am Pedro Rosales, who was on watch, spotted two violet lights, which were illuminating the ground as they descended from the sky.

Rosales informed Valdes of the phenomenon, who ordered his men to screen the fire that they had lit with blankets and then to take cover behind a low, stone wall. Next they saw a large flying object a little way ahead of them, down a slope. They observed a central light, with a smaller light on either side. Whatever it was, it was Valdes' job to find out. Praying for God's protection, he ordered his men to cover him before stepping over the wall and setting off into the darkness. After a few minutes the object disappeared.

Fifteen minutes later Valdes reappeared, stumbling into the camp from the opposite direction from which he had left as if in a trance. He was mumbling the words 'You do not know who we are or where we come from, but I tell you we shall return'. Then he blacked out. The men tended to him overnight and in the morning were shocked to see that he had grown a full beard – it was as if he had not shaved for days. His digital watch had stopped at 4.30am, but the date display said that it was 30 April – five days later.

Australasian abductions

On the night of 30 October 1967 a wool-grader named Harris, a married man with three children, had paid off his shearers at an outpost near Mayanup, Western Australia, and was driving to another station at Boyup Brook. Suddenly, on a deserted stretch of the road, the electrics in his car just cut out. 'I had no feeling of deceleration', he said. 'The car just came to a halt.'

Everything around him became quite and then a beam of blue light hit the car. It came from an oval object in the sky above and Harris had the sensation that he was being watched. Then the light disappeared and the car started working again. Again, Harris noted no sensation of acceleration: the car was just speeding down the road again. It was as if he had been momentarily frozen in time.

He later noticed that his watch, which was usually extremely accurate, had lost several minutes. Furthermore, for two weeks after the event he had a constant headache. Thinking that he was ill, Harris went to the doctor, who referred him to a psychiatrist in Perth. A medical team searched for evidence of temporal-lobe epilepsy, which can cause brief lapses of consciousness, but found none. Regressive hypnosis was not used in Australia in 1967, but even in the absence of recovered memory the Harris case bears all the hallmarks of a classic alien abduction.

Maoris and Aborigines also had similar abduction experiences. On 22 February 1969, for example, at Awanui in New Zealand, one Maori

This photograph of a UFO was taken in 1966 by Robert Rinker, a field technician from Climax, Colorado.

encountered several tall, white-skinned, blond-haired non-humans who had emerged from a big, glowing object in the woods. Before they could grab him he ran off and performed the rites used locally with which to ward off evil spirit (which apparently mainly consisted of running around in a circle while urinating).

In 1971 there had been a rash of UFO sightings in Kempsey, New South Wales, when, at around 10pm on 2 April, a 34-year-old Aborigine went into his kitchen to get a glass of water and suddenly felt himself being sucked up into the air. He passed out and later awoke outside the window, which was broken, although the bar across it remained in place. It seems that the unconscious abductee would have had to have been squeezed through a hole just 10 inches (25cm) wide.

On 27 September 1974 a 19-year-old musician and an 11-year-old boy were hunting in the Snowy Mountains when they saw a large, white light on the horizon which was giving off a low, humming noise; everything else was deadly silent. They remembered nothing more. Although no regressive hypnosis was used on him, nine years later the boy – who was now twenty – became psychic and began having dreams that relived the experience. In them he saw himself being pulled towards the humming object. Floating inside it, he was then laid onto a table and tall, thin, grey aliens attached instruments to him to see how electromagnetic fields affected his body. (For his part, the musician resisted the aliens' advances and was consequently drugged.) The aliens showed the boy a devastated landscape, which he took to be their home planet. Strangely enough, he did not recall having been afraid.

At 6.19pm on 21 October 1978 the 20-year-old Frederick Valentich flew out of Moorabbin Field, Melbourne, in a Cessna 182 (call sign Delta Sierra Juliet). According to his flight plan, he was flying to King Island, in the Bass Straits, midway between Tasmania and the coast of Victoria. He was on his way to pick up crayfish and had collected A$200 from friends with which to buy them.

At 7pm Valentich passed the coast and began his long descent. Everything was going to plan when, at 7.06pm, he radioed air-traffic control in Melbourne and asked if there were any other aircraft in the area. The air-traffic controller, Steve Robey, replied in the negative, whereupon Valentich asked if Robey had radar contact with the peculiar aircraft that he could see in his vicinity, but Robey replied that it was out of range. It was now twilight, and Valentich said that he could see a large, dark mass with four bright landing lights on it. Robey later said that Valentich had sounded scared; the craft, he reported, had flown closely overhead at great speed. Robey checked again and ascertained that no civilian or military aircraft was scheduled to be in the area.

Robey then heard Valentich say 'It's not an aircraft . . . it's a . . .', before his voice trailed off. A minute later Valentich said that the object was circling directly above him. Then, at 7.12pm, six minutes into the encounter, Valentich reported that the Cessna's engine was failing and that he was going to try to glide to King Island. The UFO was still in the vicinity: 'It is hovering and it's not an aircraft', said the panic-stricken Valentich.

The beleaguered pilot then repeated his call sign, before falling silent. His radio continued transmitting for another 17 seconds, during which time Robey heard strange noises, like metal scraping. Neither Valentich nor the Cessna were ever seen again. No wreckage was found and the accident enquiry could venture no explanation for the loss of the plane. However, there had been numerous reports of UFO activity over the Bass Straits shortly before Valentich's flight and several UFO contactees have reported that he is alive and well and living on another planet. One even claims to have seen him.

On 8 August 1993 the 27-year-old Kelly Cahill and her husband were driving through the Dandenong foothills on their way home to Belgrave, Victoria, when they saw an alien spacecraft hovering a short distance in front of them above the road. The light that it gave off was so bright that Cahill had to shield her eyes with her hand. What seemed like just moments later, she asked her husband what had happened. He did not know. When they got home they found that they had lost an hour and Cahill also discovered a strange, triangular mark around her navel.

Memories of the experience later came back to her. They had been driving around a long curve in the road when the spaceship had landed to the side of it. Cahill had told her husband to stop the car. Both of them had then got out, only to see that the spacecraft was not a spacecraft at all, but a black, 7 foot (2.1m) tall, alien creature. Although it had arms and legs like a human, its eyes were complex, like those of an insect, and glowed red. And it was not on its own: there were others nearby. A group of the aliens had approached the couple, while a second group blocked their retreat to the car. Cahill had felt that these creatures were evil and her husband had begged them to let them go. Then Cahill had been sick. The next thing that she remembered was being back in the car.

Afterwards, like other abductees, Cahill was plagued by nightmares about the encounter. She did not undergo regressive hypnosis to find out what had happened during the missing hour, but believed that one of the creatures had bent over and kissed her on the stomach, hence the mark.

African abductions

During the spring of 1951 a British engineer working in Paarl, near Cape Town in South Africa, had fixed his troublesome car himself and had then decided to take it for a test drive, even though it was late.

He was in a deserted spot halfway up Drakensteen Mountain when he decided to stop, whereupon a very short man dressed in a brown laboratory coat emerged from the shadows. He had no hair, a smooth face and a domed head. 'We need water', he said, in a strange accent. The only water that the engineer had was in the car's radiator, so he took the stranger to a nearby stream. It was then that he saw a huge flying saucer half hidden in the lee of the mountain. The alien was grateful for the engineer's help and invited him aboard. Inside, he was shown a bed, on which another alien was lying.

The engineer was not subjected to a humiliating examination, nor was he offered sex, but the alien said that in recompense for the man's kindness he would answer any questions that he had. Naturally, being an engineer, he wanted to know how the spaceship worked. In response, the alien explained 'We nullify gravity by means of a fluid magnet'. He also asked the alien where he came from, but the alien rather unhelpfully simply pointed to the sky and said 'Up there'.

Also in South Africa, in 1956 the 56-year-old Jean Lafitte was abducted by aliens with large heads and no hair. They paralysed him, before taking him into a room in which he was put on a table and medically examined. During this procedure they implanted something into his brain which would activate his psychic powers, they explained. They said that they were from the Pleiades star cluster and also told him that there was another species of alien visiting Earth from Alpha Centauri. The aliens were not hostile, they said: they had come to lend humankind a helping hand. Over the next 30 years they abducted Lafitte regularly, and in 1986, in the wake of the Chernobyl disaster, told him that they had mopped up the excess radiation spilled by the nuclear-power station.

A Rhodesian named Peter met another helpful alien in 1974, when he was driving overnight with his wife Frances from what was then Salisbury, Rhodesia – now Harare, Zimbabwe – to Durban, in South Africa. All of a sudden, on a deserted stretch of road between Umvuma and Beit Bridge, he saw lights in the sky and had the feeling that the car had been taken over by a strange force. Everything fell silent, the scenery looked unreal and the car seemed to be gliding along without touching the road. Peter then fell into a trance and lost all track of time, while Frances slept through the whole experience (maybe her sleep had been induced). Later, they realised that they had lost some time. Furthermore, the car had not used as much petrol as it should have done.

Peter was something of a veteran of close encounters. At the age of 13 he had been on a delivery run with his father, a truck-driver, when they had seen a UFO at Shabani. When they had dropped off the electrical equipment that they had been carrying it was found that all the circuits in the equipment had been destroyed by a power surge. Peter also reported having had dreams of floating, as well as out-of-body experiences.

Under hypnosis, he recalled that during the 1974 experience an alien had been beamed down into the car. Using telepathy, he had shown Peter a laboratory on an alien spacecraft in which aliens experimented on the humans that they abducted. The aliens, he said, were able to appear in any form that the witness found acceptable, and on this occasion – as on so many others – the alien had appeared as a small, hairless human with no reproductive organs.

The alien revealed that there were thousands of them living among humankind. They never interfered directly in human affairs, he claimed, but instead tried to influence individuals. He said that they had used this influence to change the world in the past and would do so again – perhaps to end war or to introduce 'their way of doing things'. Yet the alien's various explanations about where he came from were not consistent. At one point he said that he and his fellows had not travelled across space, but across time: they had 'come back in time to get to the Earth'. He also said that they came from the 'outer galaxies', as well as from the '12 planets of the Milk Way'.

In the early evening of 15 August 1981, in a heavily forested area around Mutare, on the border between Zimbabwe and Mozambique, 20 workmen were returning to their village when they saw a ball of light drifting across their path, lighting up the entire La Rochelle estate. All of the men ran for it except for Clifford Muchena, the head man, who watched as the ball turned into a glowing disc and travelled rapidly over the estate.

The light that the disc gave off was so bright that Muchena feared that it might set the forest on fire and therefore raised the fire alarm. The glowing disc then seemed to set down and three tall beings approached him; they were silhouetted in the glow and he thought that they might be estate workers, so he called out to them. This was the wrong thing to do, because they were aliens. They promptly turned towards him and zapped him with a brilliant flash that hurt his eyes. Then he was assaulted with mind-jarring force and lay dazed and paralysed for some time. When he recovered his senses the aliens and their glowing craft were gone.

Muchena seems to have experienced some missing time, but his native language did not contain the words to describe some of the key concepts needed to explain an alien abduction. (In fact, this deficiency may also be true of the English language). Furthermore, his tribe knew nothing about space travel and did not even believe that men had walked on the moon.

Asian abductions

In the late evening of 3 October 1978 Hideichi Amano, a 29-year-old snack-bar-owner from Sayama City, Japan, drove to the top of a nearby mountain, where the reception was good, to contact his brother by Citizens' Band (CB) radio. In the back of the car was his two-year-old daughter, Juri.

At the top of the mountain the car's engine cut out and the radio stopped working; next the interior began to glow. Amano stuck his head out of the window, but could see nothing; then he looked over his shoulder to check that his daughter was alright. To his horror, he saw a strange, orange light playing across her body. Suddenly he had the sensation of metal pressing against his head and looked up to see a short alien with a tiny nose. Amano was paralysed; weird images and a hideous, screaming noise flashed through his brain. When the glow disappeared the car's electrical systems began to work again, but the dashboard clock had stopped and Amano had no idea how much time had passed. Terrified, he started the car and drove away.

Although his daughter was none the worse for the experience, Amano was left with an excruciating headache. He later recalled that the alien had abducted him and had implanted something into his head, which he understood would vibrate the next time that they came to get him.

An even more disturbing tale comes from India. In a rural area in 1958, an Indian businessman and his companion saw a flying saucer land in broad daylight and four aliens 3 feet (91cm) tall get out; they seemed to have some difficulty in walking. It was later discovered that two boys who had been playing on the rock on which the alien craft had landed were missing. One was subsequently found dead and an autopsy revealed that several of his organs had been removed, as if by an expert surgeon. The other boy was found in a catatonic trance and was taken to hospital, where he survived for five days. He never regained consciousness and was therefore unable to explain what had happened to him.

Not all alien abductors in Asia are so dangerous, however. In June 1969, for example, the 27-year-old Machpud met a beautiful female alien in Bandjar, West Java. She took him back to her spaceship, where, in a brilliantly lit room, she indicated that she wanted to make love to him; he obliged. Apparently, the sex was so good that he lost consciousness, later to awake in the Gunung Babakar Forest to find his clothes distributed across a tree. Other than acute embarrassment at being found in this way by a passer-by, he suffered no ill effects.

In Malaysia, people are regularly kidnapped by the 'Bunian people' (no known human tribe). According to the Malaysian UFO investigator Ahmad Jamaludin, the Bunian are smaller versions of humans who have a unique property: during an abduction only the abductee can see them.

At 10am on one morning in June 1982 the 12-year-old Masweti Pilus was going to wash some clothes in the river behind her house when she bumped into a female Bunian around her own size. The sounds of the village faded and Masweti said that it was as if only she and the Bunian woman existed. The Bunian told her that she was going to take her to see a strange land. Masweti had no option but to go with her, yet she was not afraid and the Bunian took her to a beautiful place. She lost all sense of time, which seemed to fly by. Her relatives later discovered her lying unconscious on the ground not far from her home. Two days had passed.

Chinese people do not seem to be abducted, and perhaps with good reason. The truck-driver Wang Jian Min was driving on the road near Lan Xi, in Chekiang province, at 4am on 13 October 1979 when he almost ran into a parked car. The car-driver told Wang that he had seen a flying saucer on the road ahead and was now too scared to drive on, whereupon the fearless Wang announced that he would lead the way. The road wound to the top of a hill and Wang accordingly drove up the slope slowly. At the top was a dome-shaped craft that gave off an odd, blue glow; two silver-suited aliens about 5 feet (1.5m) tall clad were standing beside it; they were wearing bright lights – like miners' safety lamps – on their heads. Wang wondered whether he might be witnessing an optical illusion and switched off his headlights, but the aliens and the craft were still there. Determined to resolve the situation, Wang then rooted around in his truck's cab and pulled out a crowbar, but when he turned to confront the aliens with it they, along with their craft, had gone.

8 ◆ Heavenly messengers

Most alien abductors reassure their victims that they mean them no harm. Others say that they are here to help humanity and give dire warnings about pollution or atomic weapons. Sometimes, however, they also bring a positive message for humankind.

Preaching to the converted

In 1974 Betty Andreasson went public with her experience of having been abducted by aliens. The incident had supposedly taken place seven years before, on 25 January 1967, a few months after *Look* magazine had made the abduction of Betty and Barney Hill internationally notorious. Andreasson claimed that she had known nothing about the Hills' abduction until after she had been abducted herself (although her letters to her mother revealed that she had read a report of the incident, which had appeared in the Boston newspapers in 1964).

Many abductees are reticent about coming forward because they believe that others will brand them either mad or liars. For her part, Andreasson overcame any reticence that she may have had when she heard about the $100,000 that the *National Enquirer* was offering for irrefutable evidence an extraterrestrial visitor. Sad to say, she did not snatch the prize – nor did she win the $5,000 'best-case' award that went to Travis Walton 1975. Undaunted, however, in 1979 she published the book *The Andreasson Affair: the Amazing Documented Account of One Woman's Terrifying Encounter With Alien Beings*, in collaboration with ufologist Raymond Fowler.

The book told the story of Andreasson's abduction by aliens. The details of the abduction were later recovered during 14 regressive hypnosis sessions held between April and July 1977. The incident had taken place after one of a series of electrical black-outs that had plagued the north-eastern United States during the 1960s and 1970s. When the lights went out on 25 January 1967 Andreasson's six children came scurrying into the kitchen to ask what was going on. Then Andreasson saw a pinkish light outside the kitchen window; it was getting brighter, as well as pulsating. Her eldest daughter, 11-year-old Becky, saw the glow, which was now a reddish-orange, too. Everything fell silent: even the normal noises of the night disappeared 'like the whole house had a vacuum over it', Andreasson said. She became frightened and shooed the children into the living room.

Next, Andreasson's father hurried into the kitchen to find out what was happening. 'The creatures I saw through the window of Betty's house were just like Hallowe'en freaks', he said, in a sworn statement. 'I thought they had put on a funny kind of head-dress imitating a Moon man. It was funny the way they jumped one after the other – just like grasshoppers. When they saw me looking at them, they stopped . . . the one in front looked at me and I felt kind of queer.' Becky also saw the creature silhouetted against the light; after that she, along with all of the members of the family apart from her mother, found themselves unable to move. They were unaware of anything else.

The lights then came back on and four 'entities' marched into the house, passing straight through the solid, wooden door. They wore dark-blue, tight-fitting uniforms, which had an insignia on the left sleeve that resembled a bird with outstretched wings. They were about 4 feet (1.2m) tall, with large, pear-shaped, hairless heads and tiny noses and mouths. Their skin was grey and clay-like, their eyes large and cat-like; they had only three fingers. Andreasson was an accomplished artist and her sketches of the aliens accompanied the book. She was also a fundamentalist Christian and at first took her visitors to be angels. After all, she said, 'Jesus was able to walk through doors and walk on water'. Admittedly, the creatures that she saw did not fit any of the descriptions of angels given in the Bible, but the scriptures urged 'Entertain the stranger, for it may be an angel unaware'.

The leading alien introduced himself as Quazgaa; he already knew her name. Their conversation took place by telepathic means. Quazgaa was slightly different from the others: one of his eyes was white, the other black, and above his eyes he had feelers, 'like a bee'. He held out his hand. Andreasson then hospitably asked if the aliens wanted something to eat. They nodded, so she went to the fridge, got out some meat and started to cook it. Quazgaa then told her that they could not eat food unless it was burned, so she accordingly turned up the heat. When smoke started to come off the meat, however, the aliens stepped back in astonishment. 'That's not our kind of food', explained Quazgaa. 'Our food is tried by fire. Knowledge is tried by fire. Do you have any food like that?'

The devout Andreasson knew exactly what he was talking about and gave him the family Bible, whereupon Quazgaa passed his hand over it and suddenly 'other Bibles appeared, thicker than the original'. He handed out the volumes to the other aliens, who began flipping through them. She saw that each page was a pure, luminous white.

In return, Quazgaa gave Andreasson a thin, blue book. (This would have given her the incontrovertible proof of alien visitation that she needed in order to win the *National Enquirer*'s $100,000 prize had she not mislaid it. However, under hypnosis, Becky managed to confirm this part of the story.) Before she lost it, Andreasson said that she had had a chance to skim through the blue book. It was full of symbols that she did not understand, but one of the aliens told her that it was about the importance of love.

Andreasson then asked the aliens why they had come. 'We have come to help', they replied. 'Will you help us?' She wanted to know whether they had come from God; they answered that they had come because the world

These UFO's were photographed in Salem, Massachusettes on 16th July 1952.

was trying to destroy itself. Andreasson then asked how she could help. In response, they told her to follow them and reassured her that her parents and children would be alright: although they appeared paralysed, they were, in fact, just 'resting'.

Convinced, she followed the aliens, whereupon all of them whooshed through the door again, without opening it. Outside, she saw an oval craft standing on struts. (When later asked why her neighbours had not seen the huge spaceship, she said that there had been a 'haze'. Weather reports confirmed that it had indeed been misty on that night. Other witnesses, however, saw a glowing, hovering object. One man said that his car's engine had died and that when he had got out he had found himself immobilised. A lot of UFO activity was reported in the area at that time, some of it correlating with Andreasson's story.)

Andreasson was frightened of entering the strange craft, so Quazgaa made the hull transparent so that she could see inside the spaceship. She noticed an odd-looking apparatus, which, she said, looked like glass balls suspended on arms that could rotate in an inner tube. Quazgaa then transformed the bottom of the ship back into a silver-gold colour. A door opened and they entered the craft. Once inside, she felt weightless and nauseous.

The aliens cleansed her under a shower of intense light, after which she put on a flimsy, white gown. Then she was strapped down onto a table in a dome-shaped room and was given an intimate examination by silver-clad creatures. Like Betty Hill, a long needle was inserted into her navel. The aliens mentioned the word 'creation', but were disappointed when they discovered that she had had a hysterectomy. Worse still, another needle was pushed up her nose, a procedure that was excruciatingly painful. When it was removed there was a 'little ball with little prickly things on it' on the end of the needle. (Ufologists believe that this was an alien device that had been implanted during an earlier, unremembered abduction.) After that she was scanned with an instrument that looked like an eye. Other things may have happened, too – Andreasson had a severe emotional reaction while under hypnosis at this point in her tale, but she was relaxed and relieved when she related that she had been allowed to get dressed again.

Later she sat down on a chair that had plainly been made to suit human dimensions. There were a number of these chairs, each of which was covered with a plastic bubble. Air tubes were connected to her nose and mouth and the bubble was filled with a grey liquid. She kept her eyes closed while she was fed some syrupy liquid through the tube. The liquid around her vibrated and she thought that she was being transported somewhere. When the fluid had drained from the bubble she felt as though the aliens had taken control of her body. Then her eyes opened and she saw a number of creatures with black hoods over their heads.

Released from the chair, she followed the creatures out of the ship through a labyrinth of dark tunnels. Their silver suits glowed in the gloom, but their black hoods made them look as though they had no heads. There was a mirror at the end of one of the tunnels and they walked through it into a world of vibrating redness. As they floated past concrete buildings along a black track, weird, lemur-like beings clambered all over them. These had no heads – instead giant eyeballs sat on long stalks that sprouted from their skinny bodies. They climbed like monkeys and their eyes swivelled round to stare at Andreasson.

Andreasson's party moved on into a green world with lush vegetation and the creatures took off their black hoods. It was very beautiful and Andreasson saw odd creatures that she described as a cross between fish and birds. In a green city she saw a white pyramid crowned with a male head that looked like that of the Sphinx, albeit thinner. Next, she saw a giant, crystalline structure whose prisms gave off beautiful rainbows of light. In front of it stood a gigantic bird that resembled the emblem that the aliens wore on their suits; it looked like an eagle and was 15 feet (4.6m) tall. As she approached it she became hot, but then it suddenly disappeared, leaving only ashes, which then turned into a worm.

After that, she heard a voice that told her that she had been chosen to fulfil a mission. She asked whether it was the voice of God, but was told that its owner would only be revealed to her 'as time goes by'. From the things that it said, however, she soon began to believe that it was indeed the voice of God and started to cry. Andreasson was given an important message for the world. Unlike the earlier messages, which had been communicated telepathically in English, this important directive was in the aliens' own language. It was 'Oh-tookûrah bohûtûtah mawhûlah dûh dûwa ma her dûh okaht tûraht nûwrlahantûtrah aw-hoe-noe marikoto tûtrah etrah meekohtûtrah etro indra ûkreeahlah.' (That, at least, was Fowler's phonetic rendition of it. When she was later asked what it meant Andreasson said that she did not know.)

Quazgaa took pity on her and gave her a message in English to convey to humankind when she returned to Earth. The aliens loved the human race, he explained, and had come to help. But unless humans could learn acceptance they would not be saved. 'All things have been planned', Quazgaa said. 'Love is the greatest of all . . . We have the technology that man could use . . . It is through the spirit, but man will not search out that portion.' He also warned her that the human race would not believe her message until much time had passed.

Andreasson then retraced her steps though the strange, alien world. Thereafter the spacecraft transported her back to Earth while she sat in the immersion chair. Another of the aliens – Joohap, who was carrying two glowing balls – accompanied her into the house. He kindly put the children to bed before re-entering the spacecraft, which zoomed off.

That was not the end of Andreasson's contact with aliens, however. A being about 4 or 5 feet (1.2 or 1.5m) tall that appeared to be made entirely of light appeared in her house soon afterwards and leapt down the stairs.

Then, several months after her abduction, while she was washing the dishes, something took control of her mind which enabled her to see into the future. She said that she could envisage inventions made thousand of years hence, but did not reveal any details.

During the hypnotic sessions Andreasson claimed that she was still engaged in telepathic communication with one of aliens, whose name was Antonio. The ufologists present asked if they could communicate directly with him. 'You would worship him if he was to come here', she responded. 'But that is not his way. He is just a servant and a messenger.' They asked if Antonio could supply proof that he actually existed and was talking through her, to which Andreasson replied 'The world seeks proof. They cannot see with the spiritual eye. Only those worthy will see.' She then confirmed that the aliens' visitation of Earth heralded the second coming of Christ.

After the hypnotic sessions were over Andreasson divorced her husband and moved to Florida, where she married again (her new husband had also been abducted by aliens, in June 1967). They heard angry voices talking in unidentifiable languages on the telephone and Andreasson's daughter awoke one night to see a huge ball of light swoosh over her head; on the following night Andreasson's two oldest sons were killed in a car accident.

Renouncing the world

On the night of 14 December 1983 Antonio Tasca, a radio announcer from Chapeco, Brazil, was abducted by a pale-skinned beauty with oriental eyes. She told him that her name was Cabala and that she came from the planet Agali. She said that like others who had cosmic minds he had been specially chosen to 'spread the word'.

Most abductees believe that their alien abductors have hypnotically implanted the suggestion that they must forget everything that they have experienced, but not Tasca: indeed, Cabala used a machine with which to implant the message 'you will never forget' into his unconscious mind. She also gave him another token that he would not forget – burn marks on his back. 'The mysterious burns are inexplicable', said his doctor. 'They cause no pain, erythema, fever or other symptoms of first- or second-degree burning.' After his abduction Tasca lost all interest in material things.

Keeping the secret

In 1976 the 50-year-old farm-manager Ted Pratt and the 42-year-old British Rail washroom-attendant Joyce Bowles, both from Winchester, in Hampshire, were regularly visited by aliens. They were driving on the first occasion when they saw an orange glow in the sky before suddenly being pulled across the road by a strange force. The car's engine then cut out, the lights dimmed and they found themselves on the grass verge next to an egg-shaped spaceship. A tall figure, with pink eyes, blond hair and beard and wearing a silver suit, got out of it. He came over to them and leant on the car, but when Pratt and Bowles looked away he simply vanished, along with his spacecraft. Then the car's lights came on, the engine started and they drove home.

Bowles had red marks on her face for several days thereafter. She had to remove her wedding ring because the skin underneath it was sore. She also found that her watch had been magnetised and had begun to gain time.

On the night of 30 December in the same year they were driving near Winchester when they again noticed an orange glow in the sky. Although they seemed to have remembered everything about the previous alien encounter, this time there were gaps in their recollection. The next thing that they remembered was being in a room with three tall beings who spoke in a strange language. The only word that they remembered was 'mil-ee-ga', which the aliens seemed to use rather a lot.

Pratt was asked to walk up and down and to say if he felt hot or cold. The couple was then shown odd, transparent images on the walls. 'This is our field', they were told. Pratt, a farmer, assumed that they meant that it was pasture land, a misunderstanding which seemed to annoy them. Nevertheless, in order to put the abductees' minds at rest the aliens explained that they had not come as invaders. 'That's what Hitler said', commented Bowles. The aliens were offended by this, too, but still continued to impart more information to the hapless couple; sadly, most of it went over their heads.

After that there was a sudden flash of light and they found themselves back in their car on an unfamiliar road; about an hour seemed to have gone by. Bowles was psychic and said she was sure that the aliens would return. They did, but this time they appeared to her alone, giving her a message of a religious nature which she refused to divulge – even to Pratt.

The people from Janos

Apparently there was once a planet called Janos, which was located several thousand light years from Earth. It was inhabited by humans who had left Earth many thousands of years ago. It was like Earth, only nicer, in that there were no wars, work or similarly unpleasant things. Yet it seems that such an untroubled life could not go on in this paradise for ever.

Janos had two moons, both smaller than the Earth's. The one nearest to the planet was called Saton. For some reason Saton's movement slowed down imperceptibly and it gradually moved closer and closer to the surface of the planet until the tidal effect caused by the gravity of Janos ripped the moon apart and huge rocks showered down onto the surface of the planet, destroying everything.

The people of Janos had seen this disaster coming, however, and had built huge, orbiting spaceships, which were large enough to accommodate the entire population of the planet. Other, smaller ships were built in enormous, underground factories and were used to ferry the population to the vast, orbiting cities. Despite their hugely advanced knowledge of science and technology the people of Janos were caught unawares when Saton began to break up ahead of schedule. Those who were not killed outright by boulders the size of houses falling from the sky made for the underground shipyards. Ships carrying as many survivors as they could hold took them up to the orbiting spacecraft through showers of rock. Many made repeated trips, but in the end the rock showers became too severe and many Janosians had to be left to die.

The survivors on board the enormous spacecraft watched helplessly as the nuclear-power stations on the planet blew up, encircling Janos with a shroud of radioactive dust. When it was safe for rescue ships to travel to the planet's surface again they found that those who had survived the catastrophe were terminally ill with radiation sickness. They did what they could for them and the giant spaceships remained in orbit until the last of those on the surface had died. Then the traumatised survivors of this planetary disaster set out across the vastness of space – their destination a planet that they had read about in their history books: Earth.

They accelerated to something approaching the speed of light, but still the journey took thousands of years (in earthly time). When they arrived above the Earth they abducted an unassuming English family and showed it videos of the catastrophe that had befallen their planet.

The family in question consisted of John, his wife, Gloria, their daughters, five-year-old Natasha and three-year-old Tanya, as well as John's sister, Frances. On the evening of 19 June 1978 they were travelling home to Gloucester after attending a family funeral in Reading, taking the A417 via Faringdon and Cirencester, a route that they were all thoroughly familiar with.

Shortly after passing Standford-in-the-Vale they noticed a bright light in the sky which seemed to be keeping pace with the car. But John was driving at less than 50 miles (80km) an hour, which would have been impossibly slow for an aircraft. John remarked, half jokingly, that it was a UFO; he wanted to stop and have a good look at it, but they kept finding reasons not to do so. Then things seemed to become somewhat spooky: for example, they saw an illuminated house which was not there when they travelled along the same route on the following day.

John slowed down and watched the light moving ahead of them before turning back. He stopped by a hedge, but when he got out of the car the light was no longer there. Suddenly a huge, bowl-shaped craft appeared directly in front of the car, thereafter moving away to the right and sinking down behind a line of trees. He could now see a line of coloured lights along its rim. Gloria and Frances, who had stayed in the car, saw it too, and described it as looking like a flying-saucer-shaped craft: round and flat, with a domed bulge in the middle. Apart from the lights along the rim it was dull, black and featureless. Similar craft had been seen before in the Cirencester area. They next heard a weird, swishing sound and the spacecraft moved up and down several times as if it was having trouble landing. Gloria became frightened and shouted to John, telling him to get back into the car. He did so and they drove off.

From then on things became even more strange. The road – which they had travelled along many times before – seemed unfamiliar: it was narrower than they remembered and flanked by tall hedges at points where they knew that there were broad views of the countryside. The adults were uneasy. Yet there was no possibility that they had taken the wrong road: there were no turn-offs along that stretch. Their journey down this tunnel-like section of hedged-in road seemed endless; details seemed to repeat themselves and the two sides of the road looked like mirror images. The road, which they knew to be straight and flat, now curved and undulated. They had the sensation that they were floating. It was a hypnotic, dream-like experience. John felt that he was not in control of the car: if he had taken his hands off the steering wheel and his foot off the accelerator he believed that it would have continued under its own volition.

The 1 mile (1.6km) to Faringdon took between 30 and 45 minutes, yet John had been driving at a speed of between 35 and 40 miles an hour all the way. All the time the light in the sky had followed them. Suddenly they were in Faringdon. It was only a small town and after they had left it Frances noticed that although the light was still accompanying them it now seemed to blink out every time that they passed through a town or village before reappearing again. After they had passed Cirencester, 18 miles (29km) down the road, however, it disappeared completely.

They arrived home nearly an hour later than they had expected. John phoned the RAF and asked whether any experimental aircraft had been flying in the area. Extensive checks were made with military and civilian airports, but nothing airborne on that night could be found that could have accounted for the family's UFO sighting.

When Frances was leaving to go on to her own home Natasha told her that she should keep her windows tightly shut 'or you might get sucked up into a spaceship'. John and Gloria went to bed immediately, feeling rather unwell. An hour later they awoke to hear the same swishing sound that the UFO had made. For the next few days John and Gloria suffered from an unexplained itching of the skin, and when Frances went to the hair-dresser's four days later the shampoo stung her scalp. All three adults found strange marks on their bodies: they were like bruises, only more sharply defined and they did not hurt when they were prodded.

A week after the incident, when John was in bed with flu, he dreamt that he had actually entered the flying saucer. In his dream John and the others had got out of the car and had mounted a sloping, hazy beam to a doorway in the side of the ship. Once inside, they had walked along a cor-ridor that followed the curved contours of the ship. Some inner compul-sion had told John to enter a room off the corridor; the two women, who were carrying the children, also entered separate rooms.

The room that John entered was full of electronic instruments covering the walls. What appeared to be a black dentist's chair was standing in the middle of the room. Telepathic instructions told him to sit in it and restraints gripped his legs when he complied. (The position of these restraints matched the marks found on the adults' legs.) Then a thin beam of light shot out of the panel in front of him and scanned his body. When it had finished he was released from the chair. He got up and returned to the corridor, where he met up with the others, and by way of the beam the five walked down the corridor, out of the doorway and back to the car.

A few days later Frances also had a dream, which had numerous parallels with John's except that she recalled that they had entered the ship via a moving ramp. She also said she had seen aliens watching them as they entered the craft; they seemed to have been wearing tight-fitting, silver suits.

Natasha had dreams, too, in which she was examined in a room by a number of silver-clad aliens. What had disturbed her most was their eyes, which she said were 'funny'. She also began to have waking recollections of what had happened. She said that when they were leaving the ship the aliens had given them a fizzy drink which they said would help them to forget their experience; she had refused to take it, however. (Frances later confirmed under hypnosis that she had accepted a fizzy drink.)

Natasha remembered that a lady in a gold suit had come to fetch them from the car; it was she who had switched off the lights, because Daddy had forgotten to do so. The UFO had had retractable legs, Natasha said, which went up into the spaceship in a lift. When they had entered the craft she had seen a big screen that showed the road and their car below them. She said that she had been in a room full of aliens of both sexes. They had all sat down and had been gripped around the middle by some sort of safety belt. Then she had felt the sensation of the spaceship taking off.

Natasha furthermore revealed that a lady named Akilias had taken her into another room and had shown her a video of a flying saucer exactly the same as the one that they were on. The film showed the saucer flying over, and landing on, several different planets. There were 'monsters' on one of the planets: huge, naked, hairy men (which sound rather like the North American sasquatch) who were covered in mud and lived with their families in caves, sleeping on straw mattresses. She recalled having seen four types of monster: their names, she had been told, were saunuses, vonasons, fauns and phusantheases. When she sketched them they all looked distinctly humanoid. The first three were decidedly unfriendly, but the fourth, the phusantheases, appeared to be the little green men of classic UFO yore.

University lecturer and UFO investigator Frank Johnson was convinced that the family had had a CEIV – a close encounter of the fourth (IV) kind – and persuaded all of them to undergo regressive hypnosis. Over a number of sessions Frances, John and Natasha came up with a fairly consistent recollection of their abduction. What had happened was as follows.

After the car had stopped it was surrounded by fog or mist. The spaceship straddled the road, but as it was 350 feet (107m) in diameter they were still 50 feet (15m) from the bowl-shaped centre of the hull. Several shadowy figures dressed in silver suits surrounded the car – John said that there were seven. They opened the car door and when the family got out a beam of light shone down from the spaceship above. They then stood in the light and floated up the beam into the ship. Natasha saw one of the silver-suited creatures below lean into the car and switch off the ignition and lights.

They floated into the craft through an inner hatch and found themselves in the middle of a large, circular room some 150 feet (46m) in diameter. An alien ushered them to a moving ramp that led up to a balcony on which were three or four silver-suited men. One of the reception committee made a short speech of welcome. He explained that the family would first be examined to see if earthlings were the same as them, after which they would be pleased to answer any questions that the family may have. After a guided tour of the ship they would be taken back to their car and everything would be exactly the same as if they had never stopped.

After this introduction the adults were taken into separate rooms – the children remained with their mother. As in John's dream, Frances found herself in a room which contained what seemed to be a dentist's chair. She

Although not clear, this photograph shows an unidentified flying object.

was told telepathically to sit down and was assured that she would not be harmed. However, when she sat down she found herself being thrust back into the chair as if being pushed by a heavy weight. Then she was dazzled by a bright light. She began to panic, but was told to be calm; a soothing image appeared in front of her which seemed to help. It was only at that point that she noticed that there were two thin, silver-suited men in the room who were attending to the instruments that lined the walls. They were about 6 feet (1.8m) tall and had blue eyes and blond, crew-cut hair.

She was in the chair for about 20 minutes. After the examination was over she was told that there were very few differences between humans and their abductors. The human pulse rate, however, was higher (which is perhaps hardly surprising under the circumstances). The aliens said that if they settled on Earth they thought that their pulse rates would adjust themselves automatically.

Outside the examination room Frances met a bald alien who was two or three inches taller than the others. She was taken to a café area where there were around 20 aliens sitting around drinking. An alien called Uxi-aulia then introduced himself to her. He was a pilot from Janos, he said, explaining that although they had come from a planet that was several thousand light years away the journey had taken them only two Earth years. (If they were travelling close to the speed of light, according to the theory of relativity, time would slow down, so this would be perfectly possible.)

Next Uxiaulia showed her a film of people dying of radiation sickness on Janos while he explained how their planet had been destroyed. Then he showed her stills and films of how it used to be, including images of children laughing, women wearing colourful clothes and happy people boating on the lake and enjoying barbecues in the garden. Frances was particularly interested in the odd-looking fruit and vegetables that they were eating (Janosians apparently ate little meat). Uxiaulia told her that their technology was very advanced – they even had cars that floated above the ground. He also told her that they powered their ship with static electricity. For them, coming to Earth was like stepping back in time.

Suddenly he said that they would have to go – someone was coming – and the tall alien escorted her through the maze of corridors. She could hear a deep humming – like that of a turbine engine – somewhere below; then the deck pitched, knocking her off her feet. The tall alien took her into a room, where she was reunited with Gloria and the children. They sat down and waited for John, noticing that all the furniture was bolted down, like that on a sea-going ship. All around them the aliens were tapping out instructions on buttons.

John had been accompanied to the examination room by an alien called Anouxia. He seemed to be the captain, but it appeared that no one was really in charge – it was not necessary, because the ship was run by computer. Anouxia was about 6 feet (1.8m) tall, with blue eyes and a blond crew-cut. After he left John two slim, silver-clad figures entered – female aliens about 5 feet 3 inches 1.6m) tall. John was aware of the shapes of their breasts showing through their silver uniforms; their skin was soft and young-looking and they wore flimsy, silver helmets over their hair. Most of the aliens wore round badges on their chests, but the two female aliens wore similar badges, carrying flying-saucer emblems, on their belts.

Their names were Serkilias and Cosentia, they said; they already knew his name. They explained that the purpose of the examination was to see whether their race could adapt to life on Earth, from which John inferred that they planned to settle on the planet permanently. Then they strapped him into the chair and performed a number of psychological tests on him, which seemed to involve hypnosis. John also recalled the sensation of movement, as if the spaceship was taking off. When the examination was over the females told him that they had taken blood samples. After that Anouxia returned and talked to females in their own language, which was completely incomprehensible to John. Thereafter he took John on a tour of the ship. At one point they passed a porthole; looking outside, John could see only darkness. Anouxia reassured John that the members of his family were alright – they were still undergoing their medicals.

After that Anouxia and John took one of the ship's floating lifts down to the balcony where they had been greeted. In the middle of the large, circular room, John saw their car. There were also a number of pillars in the room, with square units roughly the size of a filing cabinet at the bottom of each; when Anouxia shouted into a microphone around 50 aliens ran to man these units. John looked upwards and saw that the columns supported a transparent deck, above which was a huge rotor which now began to move. Anouxia explained that if it span fast enough it acted as an antigravity machine, revealing that the rotor generated electricity at a 'very, very high voltage'. Huge cables emerged from the bottoms of the columns and inside one of the cabinets John saw a black box which could have been a capacitor. He later noticed what he took to be a giant transformer –

indeed, it seemed that the aliens powered their ship with nothing more complicated than a huge Van der Graaff generator.

Suddenly Anouxia said that John and his family had to go – someone was coming and they were frightened of being captured. Soon the rotor had sped up so fast that its blades looked blurred, causing considerable vibration and making a loud, humming noise. Like Frances, John was knocked off his feet by a jolt, whereupon Anouxia laughed and showed him the special shoes that he was wearing that kept him anchored to the floor, even when there was no gravity. John was then given an extended tour of the engine room, but it appeared to him to be nothing more than a jumble of wires and monitors. Then they took the floating lift to the navigation room, which contained a horseshoe-shaped desk from which the ship was controlled. Anouxia pushed buttons and turned knobs at the desk, but nothing that he was doing made any sense to John.

John asked Anouxia where he had come from and with the help of images shown on a screen Anouxia ran through the journey in reverse. Starting from Earth, they shot out through the solar system until Janos and its two moons eventually hove into view. Then Anouxia told John about the destruction of his planetary home; John was shown how green and fertile it had once been before seeing images of the surface of Janos strewn with huge boulders. The video probed beneath the surface of the planet, down long tunnels to underground chambers that were crammed with people who were clearly near to death, their bodily disfigurements being hidden by monks' cowls.

After showing him the video Anouxia took John to the room where the others were waiting. They were told that the spaceship was now in position and that they were about to be returned to their car. Anouxia said that they would meet again. 'When you see us again, you will know us', he promised. Then they were offered a drink to help them to forget their experience, the aliens explaining that if they remembered everything they would make their knowledge public and would consequently be exploited. With a little dose of the elixir of forgetfulness the memories would take some time to come back to them. When Natasha refused to take her drink Akilias, her minder, said that it did not matter – because she was little no one would believe her anyway.

Anouxia shook John's hand and kissed the women goodbye. They were then shown to the circular room, but their car was not longer there: instead they could see it 30 feet (9m) below them. One of the silver-clad men said that he would accompany them to their vehicle and walked out into what appeared to be thin air. The family followed him and began to descend slowly; once they were clear of the ship they could feel the breeze on their faces. They landed so gently that their knees did not even bend. The alien then told them that they would remember none of what they had seen, before floating back up to the ship, which ascended and sped away.

From his regressive-hypnosis debriefing of these five abductees Johnson put together a history of Janos and its people. The message was clear: humankind's brothers and sisters from outer space needed somewhere to live. Johnson made a rough estimate of the number of survivors of the planetary catastrophe and suggested that an island the size of either New Zealand's North or South Island could sustain them. However, as the Janosians were clearly Nordic-type aliens – space-Vikings, as Johnson called them – perhaps Iceland would be better. Either way, they have not come back to explore the possibility.

Men in black

At 5.15pm on 23 January 1976 a 17-year-old receptionist named Shelley got off the bus in Bolton, Lancashire. She was on her way home from work and had just a short walk ahead of her, across a quiet housing estate, when she saw two coloured lights in the sky which appeared to collide. Then a flying saucer the size of a house swooped down to rooftop height. The wind that it generated flattened her, after which the terrified Shelley picked herself up and ran home.

So hysterical that she could not speak, she dragged her mother into the street to show her the UFO. It had gone, however. Her mother feared that she had been raped and called the police. By the time that they arrived Shelley was calm enough to tell her story; the police concluded that she had been startled by a low-flying aircraft and left.

The day after her experience Shelley was having a bath when she noticed burn marks on her body. For the next few days she felt dizzy and sick and her eyes were sore. Her doctor diagnosed flu, but this did not explain what had happened to her fillings. During the encounter she had sensed a vibration in her mouth; it later transpired that her fillings had turned to dust and that she required emergency dental treatment.

A number of other young women reported having seen lights in the sky on the same night and the local paper decided to run a UFO story. It called the police, who told it of Shelley's encounter. Reporters beat a path to her door, but Shelley was young and unable to cope with such public pressure and therefore did not tell the whole story. She crucially omitted to mention that she had lost around three-quarters of an hour: although she had seen the UFO at 5.20pm – when she was less than a minute from home – she had not arrived at her house until 6.05pm.

During the following years Shelley had a number of psychic experiences, which often included the sensation of floating; her mother and sister also claimed to have seen her levitate. Eight years after the encounter Shelley contacted a UFO investigator, who organised hypnotic-regression sessions for her. Under hypnosis, Shelley recalled having been in a room with a female alien who had platinum-blonde hair and was dressed in a surgical gown. The word 'Babinski' then sprang into Shelley's mind. (She had no reason to know that Babinski was the name of a French neurologist who had developed a neurological test to check for spinal damage. In a healthy patient the big toe automatically extends when the sole of the foot is stimulated; this reflex is checked on new-born babies and accident victims.)

The female alien poured all sorts of ideas into Shelley's head. At some time in the future, she was led to believe, these memories would be triggered and she would be used as a messenger. She was also told that the aliens would return to see her again when 'man rises against man and nation against nation'.

The regressive hypnosis sparked nightmares concerning a holocaust and Shelley developed a morbid fear of atomic energy. She said that she was also visited by men in black suits, who tried to persuade her that the UFO that she had seen was, in fact, an experimental aircraft.

Swedish conversion

In April 1969 a Swedish hippie named Kathryn Howard was enjoying a trip to the fjords with two male friends, Martin and Harvey. Although it was a beautiful, sunny day, the conversation turned to world problems, particularly the wars in Biafra and Vietnam, which were under way at the time. Kathryn became upset when she thought of all the cruelty in the world and began to cry, whereupon she looked up to see a huge, oval UFO hovering in the sky with its landing gear deployed. Martin saw it too, but before Harvey could look skywards the UFO had vanished. The next thing that they knew was that they were at home on the sofa. It was 11pm and they had 'lost' ten hours.

Martin and Kathryn had had some sort of vision. They thought that they had seen the moon at close quarters – although the first lunar landing would not be until July, Apollo 9 had orbited the moon in March and had beamed back pictures of it. In her vision Kathryn felt herself floating and saw the Earth below her. She had the feeling that she now understood the forces of nature; hearing a slow, steady pulse, she believed that she was hearing the heartbeat of the universe – somehow it seemed that she had tapped into the 'cosmic consciousness'. She saw the whole history of the human race flash before her eyes and was overwhelmed by an intense feeling of joy. Wars, famine and diseases, she felt, were just part of the evolution of the planet, but if everyone had the insight that she had been given there would be no more human conflict.

In 1986 Kathryn underwent regressive hypnosis in an attempt to relive her vision. Under hypnosis, she recalled having seen the UFO retracting its landing gear. Then it had seemed to suck her inside it before whisking her into space – she had been terrified that she was being taken away permanently. The aliens whom she had seen on board were transparent. They had taken her to another planet, where she had seen a rocket being launched. She had been allowed revisit her past lives and had had a terrible vision of the world being destroyed in a holocaust – it was a warning to humankind.

The anti-gravity machine

In 1979 Graham Allen, a painter and decorator, was living in the wilds of Staffordshire while his fiancée, Charlotte, stayed in Maidenhead, Berkshire. At weekends they took it turns to drive to each other's house. On Friday 17 June – a sunny day – it was Graham's turn to drive to Charlotte's and he was heading along the A34 as usual. He was nearing the point at which he usually turned off on to the A423 when he heard the DJ on the radio say that the time was 5.55pm. Then the radio crackled and fell silent; he looked down at it and saw that the power light was still on. When he looked up again he could hardly believe his eyes: it was no longer bright and sunny, but overcast and teeming with rain and he had to switch on his windscreen-wipers.

Although he had driven up and down this road twice every other weekend he no longer recognised anything that he saw. He discovered why when he saw a sign saying that it was 3 miles (4.8km) to Newbury – he was therefore 20 miles (32km) past the turn-off to the A423, yet the clock on the dashboard said that it was only 6.05pm. Somehow he had covered 20 miles in 10 minutes, which meant that he would have had to have been travelling at 120 miles (193km) an hour. He certainly hadn't been driving that fast.

He pulled in to the entrance to a farm in order to turn around. The next thing that he knew was that although he was sitting in the car in the farm entrance the car was facing towards the road, which meant that he had already turned round. And the radio was now working perfectly. He was three-quarters of an hour late when he finally got to Maidenhead, but on his arrival he could not get out of the car: his legs were temporarily paralysed. This 'missing-time' experience heralded a series of bizarre dreams, which gradually subsided, however.

Over Christmas in 1987 Graham awoke at 3am and suddenly had a vision of being in his car on that day eight years earlier. He heard a low, humming sound that frightened him. There was a man on the other side of the road and Graham screamed at him for help. But it was too late: the humming intensified and the car was bathed in a golden light, whereupon it began to rise upwards. He passed out and awoke to find himself lying on his back and unable to move because three aliens seemed to be operating on him. Since then he has received telepathic messages from the aliens, including details of how to build an anti-gravity machine, which, sadly, he has not yet done.

How not to be abducted

Jason Howard was an insurance salesman who had gone back to university to work for a PhD in English literature when he became involved in Professor Jacob's abduction study. Under hypnosis he recalled having been abducted in 1976, when he was 17.

The aliens had shown him a picture of a nuclear explosion which had produced a huge, white cloud that enveloped much of the world. They had discussed the atomic bombs that had been dropped on Japan at the end of World War II and the alien had been surprised that Howard knew about it because it had happened before he was born. But the explosion that he was being shown on the screen was not something that had happened in the past, he was told – it would happen in the future. He was being given a terrifying preview of a nuclear holocaust and he must warn the world about it. It would happen one month before his fortieth birthday – in other words, in 1999.

Passing on one such dramatic message to the world via Howard was evidently not enough, for the aliens repeatedly abducted him, which became rather tiresome. Later, however, he stumbled upon one of the few effective defences against alien abduction: he discovered alcohol. When the aliens grabbed him from his college room one night he was in no mood to co-operate. Although he was happy enough to lie on the examination table, when they started fiddling about with him he got up and protested. The aliens tried to calm him down, but he would have none of it and stood unsteadily in the middle of the room making wild karate movements. The smaller aliens cowered against the wall while a tall alien tried to reason with him, but with no success because Howard was fighting drunk. The tall alien then stared deep into his eyes and the next thing that he remembered was that he was standing on the college lawn, about a mile away from his room, in his underpants.

9 ❖ Alien experiments

Most abductees report that they were given a thorough medical examination; others say that aliens implanted objects into them. Some ufologists believe that these things are being done as part of a giant, alien experiment involving human genes.

Alien evidence
Sometimes, when alien abductions are performed carelessly, the aliens leave evidence behind them. This was the case in the abduction of two teenage girls who were taken more than a decade apart.

On the night of 7 October 1955 a young girl named Jennie was tucked up in bed in Nebraska when something strange happened. She had to wait for nearly 30 years to find out what, until, in 1984, she was hypnotically regressed and recalled that a creature whom she called 'The Explorer' had come to visit her. He had been hovering outside her bedroom window telepathically willing her to come to him. She had tried to resist and had pretended that she was dreaming, but the power of his suggestion had been too strong and she had eventually asked how she could follow him. She had received the answer telepathically: the Explorer told her about his laboratory, which, she said, was like two 'dessert bowls stuck together'. She could not really envisage it, but he had nevertheless placed the concept in her mind.

Jennie's resistance was now weakened and she began to float towards the UFO; drifting through the walls of her house she even glimpsed the dirt and cobwebs in the cavity between the inner and outer walls. Once outside, she saw the UFO clearly, although the vision pulsed. As it faded she could see inside the craft and then right through it, to the car park below.

It was chilly outside, but even colder inside the UFO, like being inside a freezer. The Explorer was waiting for her in his laboratory wearing a white, surgeon's cap, while smaller creatures milled around him.. He was between 3 and 4 feet (91cm and 1.2m) tall and had a head that was shaped like an egg. His face was waxy and greyish – it looked sensitive, as if she would hurt him if she touched it. His nose was a tiny bump with two slits for nostrils and his mouth was another slit. Jennie said his eyes were slits, too – long ones, 'with nobody home'. She sensed that he was stern, but not angry – he clearly meant business.

The Explorer did not speak to her, but instead implanted thoughts into her head. She was told to jump up on to a silver table. She then asked him where they were going, to which he replied 'Nowhere'. Clamps grabbed her and held her down. Along with a helper, the alien collected samples of her hair. A blood sample then was taken using a capillary tube. She complained that this hurt, and although he pretended that he did not care Jennie knew that he did. When the examination was over he returned to her bedroom. The sole purpose of her abduction seemed to have been the collection of samples, as if human beings were something to be studied and experimented on. In the morning she awoke and remembered her abduction as having been a vivid dream. When she looked out of her window, however, she saw that the elm tree outside had been burnt. Her father told her that it had been struck by lightning, but Jennie knew better.

The aliens who abducted Shane Kurz, a 19-year-old nurse's assistant, did not set a tree on fire, but instead left muddy footprints that led from outside up to her room. At around 4am on the night in question, 3 May 1968, Shane recalled having seen a UFO. She remembered nothing more until her mother woke her in the morning; she could not explain the footprints.

Six years later she approached Professor Hanz Holzer, a parapsychologist, with her story. She was desperate: since that night she had suffered from nightmares and migraines; strange, red rings had appeared on her abdomen and she had stopped menstruating for nearly a year. Doctors were at a loss to explain her condition. Then, in February 1973, her symptoms suddenly disappeared. She still wanted to get to the bottom of what had happened to her, however, and felt that her unexplained illness was in some way connected to both the UFO and the mysterious, muddy footprints.

When Professor Holzer hypnotised her Shane remembered having been abducted from her bedroom by aliens. They were small, with grey skins, probing eyes and no hair. Having taken her to a strange room, they had then insisted that she get on to a table; she had not wanted to, but had had no choice. One of the aliens had seemed to know her, but she could not work out how. He had stuck a long needle into her abdomen and had taken samples of her ova. She was told that she had been chosen to give them a baby and that they were experimenting on her to see if she could. After that she was raped.

Professional courtesy

Given the aliens' predilection for examining human women intimately, who better to find out what they are up to than a professional gynaecologist? On 7 August 1965 a highly respected Venezuelan gynaecologist and two businessmen were visiting a stud farm at San Pedro de los Altos, 30 miles (48km) south of Caracas. During the late afternoon they were discussing horses and investments when suddenly there was a blinding flash. The three men looked up to see a glowing sphere, bathed in yellow light, drifting down from the sky. They sensed a soft humming, which seemed to be coming from inside their heads. One of the men turned to run away, but the gynaecologist grabbed him. 'Stay and watch', he said.

By this time the sphere was hovering just above the ground, but it was still a safe distance away. Suddenly a beam shot out of the side of the globe; it was angled to the ground like a ramp and two aliens then floated down it. They were 7 feet (2.1m) tall, with blond hair and huge, round eyes and their suits were made of tinfoil. The three men were terrified, but fear rooted them to the spot and they could not run. The aliens casually walked over to them. 'Don't be afraid', they said. 'Calm yourselves.'

They communicated with the men telepathically, the men hearing their voices inside their heads. The gynaecologist asked the aliens what they were doing on Earth. 'We come from Orion', said the aliens, explaining that they had come to Earth to study the psyche of humans in order to adapt them to their own species. They also wanted to experiment with the possibility of interbreeding with humans to create a new, hybrid species.

This UFO picture was taken over the Mojave Desert, California.

The aliens also helpfully unravelled another mystery – why some people report encountering tall, blond, blue-eyed, 'Nordic' aliens, while others see small, black-eyed 'greys'. They explained that there were other extraterrestrial visitors to Earth besides themselves. The short aliens were from the 'outer dipper', but their purpose was unclear. The Nordics said that their own mission was peaceful. For example, they could have brought a 'wave compressor' big enough to disintegrate the moon, but instead they had only brought a few small ones with them. Although puny, these were 'powerful enough to halt an atomic explosion' (they presumably carried them for self-protection).

The Venezuelans and the aliens then had a long, philosophical discussion, but the men's memories of what had been said later became hazy.

Mysterious bleeding

On the night of 29 April 1995 a company director named Malcolm, his wife, Samantha – a charity organiser – and their daughter, Lizzie, were driving across the south of France. They were travelling down the motorway between Epagny and Caignes Cordon, two hours from Dijon, where they intended to spend the night, when they saw a UFO, which appeared to be following them. They tried to shake it off by speeding up and then slowing down, but the only time that it disappeared was when other traffic appeared on the road. Neither Malcolm nor Samantha believed in UFOs, but after it had followed them for several hours they were forced to come to the conclusion that not only did they exist, but they were not necessarily friendly.

Although they drove for hours they did not reach Dijon that night, and at around 2am, after checking that the UFO was gone, they slept in the car. When they awoke Samantha had a nosebleed and Lizzie was bleeding from the anus. It was only when they got back to England that they realised that it had taken them three-and-a-half-hours to cover the 40 miles (64km) from Epagny to Caignes Cordon. (They later drove along the route again and ascertained that they could not have taken the wrong turning.)

After seeing the UFO all three were plagued by disturbing dreams and saw humanoid creatures with black eyes. The stress caused Samantha's hair to fall out. Nine months after the encounter Samantha awoke to hear Lizzie crying, but found that she was temporarily paralysed. Malcolm went to see what was wrong with Lizzie, but before he did so he first stopped by the window – there was someone digging up the road outside, he said. Malcolm said that he had then found a crying Lizzie looking out of the window. When Samantha could move again she also went to the window and observed people digging in the garden. In the morning, however, there was no sign either of any roadworks having been carried out or of the earth having been disturbed in the garden. Worse still, both Samantha and Lizzie were bleeding from the rectum. They believed that the bleeding was somehow connected to the UFO and that aliens were carrying out a bizarre experiment on them.

A seminal experience

The 19-year-old computer-programmer Will Parker was driving his wife, Ginny, through Virginia late one night in 1974 when he pulled into a petrol station that was closed. For some reason that he could not later explain he turned off the car's engine and lights and waited expectantly in the darkness.

Under hypnosis, he remembered that they had chatted nervously while they waited, but had had no idea what they were waiting for. Then Ginny had told him to be quiet because she had heard something: someone was out there. Indeed there was, and a small alien now appeared beside the car. Ginny was shocked and started praying, but Will was calm: he suddenly realised that he had seen aliens before. Ginny soon fell quiet and Will saw that she was asleep. Once Ginny was fully unconscious the aliens took Will out of the car. As they took him away he could only think about going back to lock the car – he did not think it safe to leave Ginny alone in there.

Four or five aliens were waiting at the back of the service station; 'Where are the rest?' asked Will. Telepathically, the aliens told him not to be afraid: they were not going to hurt him. They promised that they would bring him back and told him not to worry about Ginny – she would remember nothing. They were standing together in a tight group, waiting, when an alien spacecraft about the size of a building appeared. They were next lifted up as a group, although Will did not know how, and suddenly found themselves inside the spacecraft, with the Earth beneath them.

An alien pushed its face into Will's and he had the impression that it was scanning his mind. Next, they fitted a machine over his genitals, whereupon it vibrated and Will felt semen being sucked out of him; he had no orgasm or sense of pleasurable release, however.

Harvesting foetuses

In 1979 Tracy Knapp, a 21-year-old musician, was driving from Los Angeles to Las Vegas with two girlfriends when they saw a light swooping down at them from the sky.

Under hypnosis, she remembered that as the light had whizzed past the car had started spinning, whereupon all three of them had started screaming and crying. The car was being lifted up into the sky when Knapp remembered seeing hands coming in through the window. When they touched her she became limp and they lifted her out of the car. From then on she lost sight of the other women and did not see them again until they were back on the ground.

She recalled lying down with her legs pointing upwards; two creatures were pressing on her and one was cutting her internally with long-handled scissors that had very small blades. They then dowsed the wound with a fluid that burned her. The procedure continued for a long time. The aliens seemed to have been cutting threads before pulling out their instruments and removing a sac containing a tiny foetus. This was put into a small, silver cylinder about 3 inches (7.6cm) wide, which was in turn put into a drawer in the wall, along with numerous other live foetuses.

Sisters in space

Janet Demerest, a secretary, and her sister, Karen Morgan, the owner of a public-relations firm, suffered numerous abductions. The first was in 1963, when Demerest was nine. On the occasion in question she remembered having been playing near her house with some of her fellow Brownies; the other girls formed a circle, but Demerest wandered away on her own. Under hypnosis, she recalled having seen a man with grey skin; he was not very tall – only about the same height as she. Together they walked into the woods holding hands, which reassured her. She then saw a UFO landing in a clearing and she and the alien walked into it up a ramp.

Inside the craft she was led to a large room in which there were a human woman and an odd-looking girl, who had greyish skin, thin arms and long, slender fingers; she seemed to have no bone structure and no ears. The man wanted Demerest to play with her, so they sat down together on the floor. While Demerest was trying to think of a game to play, the girl just stared at her. Demerest found her stare riveting and could not pull her eyes away from it; all of the time she was aware of the man and woman watching her. Eventually the girl hugged her and told her that it was time to go. The man then took Demerest back.

When Karen Morgan was 38 she also recalled having had an abduction experience, 6 years earlier, in 1981. Under hypnotic regression, she remembered having entered a UFO and having been taken to a waiting area where there were a number of benches in arched alcoves. She sat in one and saw that there were other men and women waiting in the others. Some wore night clothes; one young man was slumped as if he was not well; another woman looked very frightened. They were then strapped in and Morgan had to tell herself not to panic; she had the curious feeling that she had been through all this before. Then the aliens came, two per human. The first woman was stripped and they were all herded into an examination room; the sick man had to be helped.

Morgan tried to resist, but the aliens pushed her along anyway. She was the last into the examination room, in which there were four operating tables and a shelf with instruments on it running around it. She was stripped and strapped to the table. (Demerest recalled having had a similar experience, but said that she had not really had a sense of what was happening or of who she was). Morgan had braces on her teeth at the time, which fascinated the aliens, who asked her to take them out. She refused, but when she awoke the next morning she found them lying on her stomach.

The aliens also cut out a sample of her gum for analysis, which infuriated her. She asked how much more of her they were going to take and how long it took to study someone. Their answer was that it could take years. A tall alien then asked her to look into his eyes; she did so and immediately felt that she was being overwhelmed, as if she was falling into them. Her will-power had been sapped and she found that she could not look away or fight the alien in any way – it was as if she no longer had a mind of her own.

Morgan later became angry about the gynaecological procedures that the alien was performing on her and cursed the creature in her mind. The alien read her thoughts and reassured her that she would come to no harm. He then carried out what seemed to be a smear test, but she believed that they were inserting an embryo into her, implanting it into her womb. She found this idea repulsive and told the alien that he could not do this, but he replied that she had no choice: it was part of a very important programme. Still she protested, however, saying that once she was back on Earth she would have an abortion, to which the alien countered that she would not because she would not remember the embryo having been implanted into her. Although she kept insisting that she would, she nevertheless sensed the alien's hypnotic suggestion that she would forget the incident overwhelming her mind. There was nothing to worry about, the alien reassured her: they had done this many times before.

Morgan then remembered that she had indeed been through this procedure many times before. She felt sick, comparing herself to an animal that was being experimented upon. The embryos, she knew, were hybrids: part human, part alien. Sometimes the procedure was quick, but this time it had taken longer because she had resisted. When the alien had finished he pulled his instruments out of her body and patted her on the stomach. Morgan was disgusted and told the alien to take his hands off her; he reluctantly did so, shaking his head as if bewildered by her unco-operative attitude. In the morning, Morgan awoke in her own bed. On feeling a mysterious, gooey substance between her legs she took a shower and washed it off.

Demerest recalled having undergone a similar procedure in 1987, when she was 33. A long needle had been inserted into her vagina and the aliens had implanted a 'little round thing' into her womb. Afterwards a female alien had helped her off the table. She had been left with the overwhelming feeling that she wanted to have a baby.

Morgan was given a glimpse of the results of her labours when she was 32, when she was shown a large number of babies – 50 or even 100 – lined up in boxes behind a glass panel. They were not moving and looked as though they were dead, although Morgan knew that they were alive. They seemed to have been suspended in some sort of liquid and were being fed through tubes by a machine. Although some were only foetuses they appeared to be in all stages of development. It seemed clear to Morgan that the aliens were running some sort of breeding programme and that these were foetuses that had been taken from hundreds of women. She was also shown nurseries, in which babies were being tended by aliens; some of them, she was told, were hers.

Morgan was sometimes told to wash a baby, or else to play with it, and saw other women (who were naked) doing the same thing. Morgan had the impression that the intention was for the babies to be touched as much as possible, but they were very unresponsive and did not even laugh or smile when they were tickled. When the women made baby noises to them the children did not make a sound.

In 1987 Morgan, along with the other humans whom she had seen tending the children, was shown in a film what would happen to the babies. It depicted an idyllic landscape – like a park, with a stream running through it – and she was told that this was where the aliens were taking the babies. At first she thought that the place was on Earth, but as the camera panned the panorama she realised that although the trees, rivers and canyons were like those on Earth they were not quite the same. The narrator explained that this was how the world would be some time in the future, when their programme was complete. Morgan suddenly felt that she did not want to look at the film any more – it was as though the aliens were trying to implant something into her mind – but she was unable to avert her eyes from the screen.

On another occasion when Morgan was abducted – when she was 30 – two aliens had lifted her up from the examination table and had held her at a strange angle. They had told her to look at a picture, but there was no screen or picture in the conventional sense – the picture was inside her head. She saw mother dying of cancer in her uncle's home, with all her relatives standing around the bed saying the rosary. It was as if the aliens had filmed it; she could even see herself standing at the back. Morgan asked why she had to watch this and one of the aliens said that they wanted her to feel it again. But reliving the experience of watching her mother die was too painful and Morgan became angry and tried to fight it – it was as if the aliens wanted to see her suffer.

During another abduction she saw an attractive man whom she knew and had the distinct impression that she was going to make love to him before gradually realising that the man was, in fact, an alien who had staged the erotic scene by means of hypnotic suggestion.

Abducted by a grey deer

Virginia Horton was a corporate lawyer who lived on the USA's east coast. She was married, with a family, and had an ordinary, everyday life. In 1979 friends told her that there had been an item on the NBC nightly news about the Bershad abduction. It was then that she remembered strange things happening to her in the past.

In the summer of 1950, when she was six, she had been on her grandfather's farm in Manitoba. She remembered that she had gone to the barn to collect eggs. The next thing that she remembered was that she had been in the yard again. She had felt an itch on the back of her calf and had pulled up the leg of her jeans see what was causing it. It turned out to be a neat and surgical wound, as if it had been cut with a scalpel, but there was no hole in her jeans and she did not understand how it could have happened.

She now asked her mother about the incident, but she did not remember it. However, she did recall another strange event that had occurred when Horton was 16. They had been holidaying in France and were having a picnic in the countryside when Horton and her brother had gone off to explore a nearby forest. They had become separated and her brother had been searching for her for about half an hour when she had suddenly reappeared, with her dress splattered with blood. She had had no explanation for this and had claimed that she had been gone for no time at all. When pressed, however, she had remembered meeting a beautiful deer.

Horton then contacted the ufologist Budd Hopkins, who arranged a regressive-hypnosis session for her. It was then discovered that when she was Manitoba she had been taken into a bright room in a spacecraft by grey aliens. They had said that they were from far way among the stars and that they just wanted to take a little piece of her back with them. She remembered that some type of apparatus on the end of a retractable arm had been used to make an incision in the back of her leg.

In the woods in France she had seen a deer – a *grey* deer, which had large, black, hypnotic eyes. (Hopkins concluded that the deer was a cover story that had been implanted into her mind by the aliens in order to cover their tracks.) She again remembered having been on a spaceship; the same aliens whom she had seen when she was six were also there. They had shown her a star map and had told her that they were from another galaxy. Then they had given her a lecture on the importance of ecology, bio-diversity and the preservation of endangered species, including the human species – all advanced ideas in 1960. They had also taken her for a short trip in their flying saucer, in which they had ascended upwards for 100 miles (161km) or so. She had been examined on a table and they had stuck an instrument up her nose which had given her a nosebleed, thereby explaining the blood on her dress.

This UFO has been photographed hovering above the Los Angeles skyline.

Put to the test

In 1965, when attorney George Kenniston was 16, he recalled having been abducted in order to act as the navigator of an alien spacecraft. On the bridge, he had followed orders, but had had no idea how he knew what to do. He remembered that he had been undergoing some sort of test: he had been taken to a complex control panel and had been told to operate it. The aliens had given him a destination and he had been supposed to fly the ship there; they had scrutinised him closely while he did so. It had been an almost impossible task, like driving for hundreds of miles in a straight line.

When the test was over Kenniston had floated down from the spacecraft, flying over the town and landing on a hill behind his home. After walking home he had let himself in through the kitchen door and was making his way to his bedroom when he bumped into his father. Kenniston told him that he had got up for a glass of water and then went back to bed.

10 ◆ Multiple abductions

The details of an abduction are frequently hidden from the conscious mind. When abduction experiences are investigated during regressive hypnosis many abductees discover to their astonishment that they have taken on numerous occasions throughout their lives.

Abduction at Copley Wood

Debbie Tomey was a mother of two in her early thirties. Following a divorce she had moved into her parents' house in the Indianapolis suburb of Copley Wood. After having closed the pool-house door on the night of 30 June 1983 she noticed that it had opened again and that the light was on inside – when she looked later the door was closed and the light had been switched off, although none of the family had been near the place. Furthermore, a bright light seemed to be hovering over the bird-feeder in the garden. Fearing burglars, and carrying her father's .22 firearm, she went out to investigate, but found nothing untoward, except that the dog was cowering the back of the car and had to be coaxed out. There was patch of burnt grass in the garden, around 8 feet (2.4m) in diameter, from which a straight path ran, ending in an arc about 50 feet (15m) away. The dog would not go near the area and the birds avoided the bird-feeder.

Like Virginia Horton, Tomey had a scar on the back of her calf – in fact, two; one of them had appeared when she was about 13. Her sister, Laura, and mother each had identical scars, but none of them knew how they had got them. Her sister had reported seeing a UFO when she was a teenager and also had the feeling that she was missing some time. When Laura was hypnotised in order to help her to lose weight she had emerged traumatised and had had to be sedated. And both Tomey and her mother suffered from the same, recurring nightmare, in which they were being terrorised by small, grey aliens. Tomey furthermore recalled that when pregnant she had been plagued by weird phone calls, in which the caller had made odd, guttural sounds, as well as clicks and moans. The calls had persisted, even though she had changed her number and had gone ex-directory. Other people – including her mother and best friend – had heard them, too, but they had suddenly ceased when the baby was born.

Under hypnosis, Tomey remembered having seen a light and having gone into the garden on the night in question. Aliens had then abducted her and had performed a number of medical experiments on her, including implanting a small device into her body. She recalled having met a child which she believed was hers – the result of an earlier abduction. When the experience was over she had woken up in the garden, bleeding.

Regressive hypnosis revealed that she had been abducted on numerous other occasions. When she was a child, her mother – who was a victim of alien abduction, too – would hide her in a cupboard in an attempt to protect her.

Tomey recalled having been abducted from a car in December 1977 (the other people in the car had been 'switched off' and therefore could not corroborate her account). She then remembered having undergone a gynaecological examination (abduction expert Budd Hopkins believed that she was impregnated by the aliens on this occasion). When she was a few months pregnant she had been abducted again, and during the subsequent examination had felt a terrible pressure inside her. Then, under hypnosis, she screamed out 'It's not fair. It's mine'.

She later began dreaming that she had given birth to an odd-looking, super-intelligent, hybrid baby. (Similar dreams of abductees giving birth to super-intelligent children – so-called 'wise babies' – soon began appearing in UFO-related literature.) Tomey revealed that all of the female members of her family had been abducted on several occasions. During these abductions they would be stripped and forced to lie on an examination table with their feet in stirrups while small, grey aliens examined them internally, either manually or by means of a needle-shaped laparoscope inserted through the navel. The aliens would sometimes implant something into the women or, at other times, remove something. Tomey also believed that her son would become another victim of repeated alien abduction.

In November 1983 Tomey reported having been abducted once more; this time the aliens had removed some of her ova. When she was subsequently abducted, in April 1986, she was shown two elf-like infants, which she was allowed to hold and name. These were her children, the aliens said, who were presumably trying to encourage her to forge some sort of mother-child bond. The aliens told her that they had nine of her offspring altogether. Tomey realised that the aliens had been impregnating her with alien genes and had then been harvesting the foetuses, which were incubated elsewhere. During one of her abductions she met another of her half-alien offspring – a slim girl, with a huge head and no eyebrows or eyelashes. Even though she looked strange and unearthly, Tomey could not help but feel a twinge of maternal affection for her.

Tomey believed that alien impregnation of human women was quite a common phenomenon. In one case a 13-year-old girl had become pregnant, even though she had protested that she had never slept with a man. Her parents, not unsurprisingly, did not believe her, but when they sent her to the doctor for an abortion the doctor reported that her hymen was still intact.

Abducted to an alien base

Christa Tilton was another victim of multiple abductions. She first remembered being taken at the age of ten, when she was visiting her aunt's house in Tucson, Arizona. Walking down a road there, she noticed a huge, orange ball of fire falling to the ground. Directly afterwards, she saw a small, grey creature, with a big head, large eyes and a thin body. She began playing with it, exchanging rocks, before blacking out. She woke up on a table with someone standing over her. This, she was told, was the 'doctor' and she would always remember him. Although he was an alien, he was very human in appearance. He gave her a thorough examination; skin samples were taken and her abdomen was probed with a long needle; a sharp instrument was also inserted into her ear.

This was the first of many subsequent abductions, during the course of one of which she believed that she had been impregnated by aliens. (The foetus was then removed from her womb during an abduction from New Orleans in 1971.)

Under hypnosis, she recalled an abduction from Arizona in July 1987 that stood out from all of the rest. She had been driving through the desert when she had seen an alien sitting on a hill. She had stopped the car, whereupon two other aliens had attacked her. Although she had locked the car doors they had still managed to unlock them, and as she struggled they had manhandled her into their waiting spacecraft. Inside the craft, she was given something to drink, which knocked her out.

When she woke up she found herself being led out of the ship, which had landed at the entrance to a cavern. This, she later discovered, was an underground alien base. There were numerous security checks; on one level her alien escort had had an argument with one of the guards, but she did not understand what it was about. As usual, she was given a thorough examination by the aliens. When it was completed she was taken down to level six, but she was not allowed into it because, as her escort explained, there were things on that level that she would not be able to understand and that might upset her.

After this seemingly fruitless trip the aliens returned her to ground level before transporting her to her car. It was now late, and she drove to her aunt's house and went to bed without disturbing her aunt or her best friend, who was staying with her. On the following morning her friend pointed to the long, red, scratch marks on Tilton's back. These, Tilton maintained, were the result of struggling with the aliens when they were trying to abduct her.

Tilton lectured regularly on her abduction experiences, which continued unabated.

'Why do you keep taking me?'

A 32-year-old nurse called Alex, who had no interest in UFOs or science fiction, reported a bizarre experience on 2 July 1997. It had been her day off and she had been relaxing in a field in the sunshine when she had suddenly felt herself being sucked up into the sky. Above her, she had seen a huge, triangular craft. Then she had blacked out.

When she awoke she was lying naked on a table in an operating theatre. She could not move, although there seemed to be nothing restraining her. She saw a number of small creatures with big heads – 'like babies before they are born' – around her. She noticed a teenage girl, who was also naked, lying on another table. Then a taller creature, with black eyes, came in. When he bent over the table she had the feeling that she had been seeing things that she should not have seen; she then went back to sleep. The next thing that she knew was that she was back in the field, but some yards from where she had been sitting. The book that she had been reading had been flung aside, into a bush. There were strange marks on her arms. Her watch had stopped, and when she got home she discovered that five hours had passed.

Thereafter she began to have a weird effect on electrical appliances. She found it difficult to sleep, but when she eventually did so her dreams were full of aliens and spaceships. She also had nosebleeds. Up until then she had been a country girl, but she soon moved to a city in order to be near people.

Under hypnosis, she related the story of her abduction, this time adding some more details. The tall creature, she said, had told her to be calm: everything that they were doing was for her own good. But she still protested. 'Why do you keep taking me?' she asked. The UFO investigator then plumbed her memory for earlier encounters. She said that she had first been abducted at the age of five, when a band of ugly children whom she had met in the woods took her to a circular house to play, but she did not want to play with them because they were too ugly.

In the following year they had come to get her again; this time she had been examined by a doctor. Then, when she was 14, she had been out with her dog when she had been sucked up through the air into an alien space-craft. This time she had found herself naked, lying on a table; samples had been taken from her and she had been told that she would not be able to bear children. When she was returned to the wood her dog had gone; it turned up two days later, but refused to go near the woods.

She was again abducted at the age of 18; that time she had seen a large room in which lots of naked women were lying on tables. At the age of 27 she had found herself unexpectedly pregnant; when she was abducted shortly afterwards she had found herself in a room containing lots of foe-tuses in large jars full of liquid. She had later lost the child and claimed, under hypnosis, that the aliens had taken it away from her. The aliens abducted her again when she was 30, but this time they only took samples of her hair, skin and fingernails.

Phantom pregnancy

Sharon, a woman in her thirties, heard the UFO investigator Tony Dodd talking on the radio about alien abduction and phoned in. She told him that although she had no recollection of having been abducted by aliens she had experienced many of the strange phenomena that plague abductees. For example, electrical equipment malfunctioned around her. Her car inexplicably stalled on lonely roads, only to restart again. She had had 'missing-time' experiences and her clocks seemed to run backwards. She had suffered from mysterious discharges from her navel and, after exhibiting all the symptoms of pregnancy for three months, had found that she was not pregnant at all. She had found blood on her pillow on several occasions, although she had no visible wound. She had woken up in different parts of the house, although she had no history of sleepwalking. Mud and grass were once found in her bedroom. And one morning she had woken to find that the nightdress that she had put on the night before had gone – it was nowhere to be found.

Under hypnosis, she revealed that she had seen huge UFOs outside her window, which had terrified her. Inside them, she said, had been big, white rooms filled with tall aliens with round heads and big eyes. They had taken her aboard regularly and had told her that they had come to help humankind look after the Earth.

During one abduction, when she was a small child, Sharon had found herself in room with a number of other people. She could see the distant Earth outside. They were given a lecture about ecology and pollution before being marched off into separate rooms. She then found herself lying down, possibly floating. There were small creatures around her, with four, long fingers, who gave her some sort of injection; a circle of gold light had made her feel elated and happy. Then she was allowed to dance and play until a big man told them that it was time to go home. When she was eight the big man again came to take her to the spaceship. Afterwards she thought that she could fly and broke her arm trying to launch herself off a slide.

At the age of 14 she was abducted from the back garden of her aunt's house after she had slipped out to have an illicit cigarette. On this occasion she was taken to a different ship, which was covered in Egyptian hieroglyphs. She remembered having been undressed and examined. Later she was again told about respecting the environment, as well as about the pyramids and spirituality. Energy, she said, was pumped into her body; it gave her pins and needles but made her feel good. Indeed, her abductors always made her feel good, but they also made her feel alone – isolated from everyone else – as if she were something special or different.

They came again when she was 22 and pregnant. The aliens placed the naked Sharon on a table, saying that they were going to check the baby, which made her anxious. They stuck a probe into her and pronounced the baby to be fine – they said that it was a girl and that it was going to help them just as she had. When Sharon was 24 they abducted both her and her daughter, Louise. Sharon was given the usual physical examination while Louise was taken to another room. They then performed a strange proce-dure on Sharon, which, they said, would cure her. When Louise returned she called one of the aliens 'Mummy'.

The next time that Sharon recalled having been abducted was when she was 33. By then she had had a hysterectomy. Her husband was asleep beside her in bed when the aliens took her onto the balcony, where there was a light that she had to walk into. She told them that she had nothing to give them – no ovaries or womb, which, she felt, were the only things that they valued her for. They replied that that was not what they had come for. When she tried to resist them they pushed her on to the examination table and shone the golden light on her, which, for the first time, made her feel guilty.

Lifetime abductee

Patti Layne, a high-school teacher, was abducted several times during her life. The first time appeared to have been when she was 15 years old. She was on a camping trip with her school when she and eight other students went skinny-dipping in a reservoir. A light approached them from the sky and then shone directly onto them, whereupon they were lifted into the UFO.

Layne was abducted again in the following year. This time the aliens told her that they needed some parts from her that would help everyone on the planet. They took her to a small room; she could see the stars and space from its window. The aliens then sat her on a chair and attached some kind of apparatus to her head which played terrible images of nuclear war, the destruction of cities, devastating earthquakes, mountains collapsing, the sun turn-ing black, people starving and her own family struggling to sur-vive. All this would happen, the aliens said, because humankind could not stop being greedy. Afterwards one of the aliens looked deep into her eyes – it was as if he was looking into her soul, she said. Then he told her to forget everything that she had seen; the next day she would think that she had just had a bad dream. At school the next day she was haunted by the awful fear that there was going to be a nuclear war. And for many years afterwards she dreamt of a nuclear holocaust.

Layne was next abducted in 1982, on her twentieth birthday, when she was studying at a college in a small town in Pennsylvania. She had decided to go for a drive in the mountains and on reaching a wild spot she turned off the road and began following a dirt track. All the time she was thinking that she should not be there – she had a class that night and was supposed to be studying. Then the car stopped; she waited for a while and it started again. Or at least that's what she thought had happened – under hypnosis, she recalled the car door having been opened and aliens taking her out.

A year later, when she was still at college, she and her friends went into the mountains for a picnic. They spread out blankets to sit on and started drinking wine. Shortly thereafter Layne wandered off into the woods to relieve herself and was squatting down in a clearing when a light was shone at her. She thought that it was Freddy, one of her friends, who was always playing practical jokes. 'Cut it out', she yelled. To her surprise, however, she could not hear her own voice; nor could she hear the others, even though they were quite close, just down the trail. She then became scared and walked back to the picnic spot, only to see a large band of aliens grabbing at her friends. One of them, James, looked ill; the others were being examined with some kind of instrument.

The aliens were small and had no genitals; they seemed to be wearing some sort of military insignia, which resembled a bird. One of them came over to her – he looked friendly and took her by the arm, like a boyfriend would. With the rest of their friends apparently having been frozen, Layne and James were marched off. Two of the aliens practically had to carry James, who looked as though he was going to vomit. They were then taken deep into the woods, where a craft was waiting; it was not a conventional flying saucer, but looked more like a black bubble, with a hatch opening into it and a row of windows around the top. It was light inside and they walked into it up a small ramp. Layne was taken into one room, James into another. One alien pressed its face to hers, as if scanning her mind. She felt

UFO's as depicted in the screen adaptation of HG Wells' novel War of the Worlds.

a deep sexual bond with him and empathised with his mission, even though she did not know what it was. The alien, she thought, was tapping into her mind, but this was not an unpleasant sensation – in fact, it was rather pleasurable.

Layne was abducted from her bedroom in 1985, when she was 23. On that occasion she recalled having had strong feelings for a tall alien and had been saddened when he had told her that it was time to go home – she had wanted to stay with him. He had assisted her off the table and his colleagues had picked up her clothes and had helped her to dress. The tall alien had then led her down a corridor and shortly thereafter they had entered a wood. The alien had walked Layne home in the moonlight. When they reached her house Layne had floated through the bedroom window and had then found herself back in bed with her husband. She had shaken him awake and had told him that she had had a strange dream, but he had just fallen asleep again. In the morning she found that the aliens had put on her nightdress inside out.

11 ❖ Bedroom visitors

Although many alien abductions take place on lonely roads and at other deserted spots, under hypnosis many abductees realise that at night their bedrooms are teeming with alien visitors who are ready to carry them off whenever they feel like it.

Communion

The book – and subsequent film – *Communion* made Whitley Strieber the world's most famous abductee. In it, he claimed to have been the victim of multiple abductions. In fact, during his whole life, he said, he had been plagued by little, bug-eyed aliens stomping around his home at night and whisking him off for proctology practice.

Strieber, the son of a wealthy lawyer, was born in San Antonio, Texas. As a child he had been fascinated by the 'space race' and once, as a joke, his school friends had painted him green because he was always talking about little green men. He later graduated form the University of Texas and went to film school in London. Then he moved to New York, where he worked in advertising, although he spent much of his free time studying witchcraft and mysticism.

In his thirties he decided to become a writer, and in 1978 published the book (which was later made into a film) *The Wolfen*, which was about a pack of super-wolves who roamed Manhattan ripping people's throats out. The Wolfen was followed by The Hunger, which told of a romance between a couple of high-school vampires. He continued writing horror-thrillers with supernatural overtones. In one book, *Cat Magic*, the female protagonist was abducted by 'fairies' – small humanoids who had 'sharp faces with pointed noses and large eyes' – who took great delight in examining her, both physically and mentally. Another common trend in his fiction was his claim that his books were true stories related by fictional characters. But in the futuristic book *Warday*, which Strieber co-wrote with James Kunetka, the two authors wrote autobiographically, fictionalising only their future experiences. The line between fact and fiction had therefore become well and truly blurred.

Then it happened. On 4 October 1985 Strieber, his wife, Anne, and their son, Andrew, along with their friends, Jacques Sandulescu and Annie Gottlieb – who were both writers – went to stay in the Striebers' cabin in upstate New York for the weekend. It was foggy that night and Strieber lit the stove before going to sleep. He awoke to see a blue light shining on the ceiling. He became frightened; the party was in the woods and therefore could not see the headlights of passing traffic and in his sleepy state it occurred to him that the chimney might be on fire. Then he fell into a deep sleep.

He was later awoken by a loud bang, which also woke his wife; he could hear his son shouting downstairs. When he opened his eyes he saw the cabin was shrouded in a glow that extended into the fog. He cursed himself for having fallen asleep, thinking that the roof was on fire. He told Anne that he would get Andrew and that she should wake the others. Before he could go downstairs, however, the glow suddenly disappeared. In the morning Sandulescu mentioned that he had been bothered by a light during the night, but nothing more was said about it.

During the course of the following week Strieber found himself becoming increasingly disturbed by the incident. Then he remembered having seen a huge crystal, hundreds of feet tall, standing on end over the house. It was this that had emitted the strange, blue glow. Anne thought that he was crazy.

The cabin gradually became a dark and terrible place in Strieber's mind. New York City also seemed dangerous, so he decided to move back to Texas. Strieber and his wife accordingly went house-hunting in Austin in November 1985, but when he saw the house that they intended to buy he became paranoid: the huge Texas sky, he thought, was a living thing which was furthermore watching him. He therefore cancelled their plans to move to Texas, to the fury of his wife; if he did not pull himself together, Anne said, she would leave him.

Strieber managed to put aside his fears and they visited the cabin again at Christmas. On the night of 26 December 1985 he awoke in the middle of the night to hear a peculiar sound, as if lots of people were running around downstairs. Suddenly a small figure rushed at him and he lost consciousness. After that he had the impression that he was being carried and woke to find himself lying in a small depression in the woods. He was paralysed, and someone was doing something to the side of his head. The next thing that he knew was that he was travelling upwards, high above the forest.

The terrified Strieber then found himself in a messy, circular room, with small creatures scurrying about around him. They first inserted a needle into his brain and then they examined his rectum with a probe, possibly taking samples of faecal matter, but leaving Strieber with the impression that he was being anally raped. After that they cut his forefinger.

Strieber awoke in his bed in the cabin feeling distinctly uneasy. He read a report in the newspapers about a UFO having being sighted over upstate New York that night. His brother had given him a book about UFOs for Christmas which he tried to read, but which inexplicably frightened him. He ploughed on, however, until he finally got to the chapter about alien abductions, and then everything began to make sense.

Back in New York City, Strieber looked up the UFO expert Budd Hopkins' phone number in the telephone directory. On calling him, Hopkins suggested that he investigate the events of the night of 4 October 1985, when there had been other witnesses. Strieber did so. His wife remembered having been woken by the bang, but did not recall the glow. Sandulescu remembered the light, but neither of them could come up with an explanation for it. Strieber's son had the most interesting recollection: when he had heard the bang he had been told that it was alright because his father had just thrown a shoe at a fly. Strieber then asked his son who had told him this. 'A bunch of little doctors', Andrew replied. He had dreamt that the diminutive doctors had carried him on to the porch and had told him telepathically that they were not going to hurt him. The boy said that it was a strange dream because it was 'just like real'.

At Hopkins' suggestion Strieber, who had been feeling suicidal, went to see a therapist, who suggested that they try regressive hypnosis, as well as therapy. After a couple of weeks Strieber dropped the therapy, but kept on with the hypnosis.

During the first hypnotic session Strieber was regressed to the night of 4 October. He recalled having noticed something flash past the window before seeing the light. In the corner of the bedroom he had seen a goblin, wearing a cloak, which had rushed at him and had struck him on the forehead with a wand. At this point Strieber screamed so loudly that he came out of the hypnotic trance; when he was put under again he saw images of the world blowing up. 'That's your home', said the goblin.

After that he saw his son in a park, an image that Strieber associated with death. The goblin said that he would not hurt Strieber and then took a needle and lit the end. It exploded, whereupon Strieber began to think of the house burning down. It was as if the goblin had implanted the image into his mind. After that he came out of the trance again, but was hypnotised once more in order to discover what had happened. This time he saw his son lying dead in the park. Then he watched his father dying: he was sitting in an armchair, choking, while his mother looked on – but this was not the deathbed scene that his mother had described.

In a later session Strieber was regressed to the night of 26 December. He recalled having been naked while being pulled from his bedroom by aliens wearing blue overalls. They had dragged him into the woods and had seated him on a chair, which had then propelled him hundreds of feet upwards, into the air. Next he was sitting on a bench in a room in the company of a female alien dressed in a tan-coloured suit. She then pushed something resembling a penis up Strieber's rectum and told him – in a flat, Midwestern accent – that he was the 'chosen one', but he scoffed at her. After that she tried to encourage him to have an erection, but he could not comply (perhaps because she had leathery, yellow skin and a mouth like an insect). The next thing that he knew was that he was lying naked on the living-room sofa; he went upstairs, put on his pyjamas and went to bed.

Further hypnosis revealed more bizarre abductions. On one occasion he had been in spaceship and had seen his sister, wearing a nightdress, sprawled on an examination table. His paralysed father had stood beside her. Lying on other tables were unconscious soldiers in uniform. He had even been invited to give a lecture on the evils of the British Empire. Another time he had woken up to find a group of hybrids standing around his bed. The aliens seemed to be tinkering with his mind, showing him symbols and images that evoked thoughts and memories in his mind.

Outside hypnosis, Strieber's life became more and more bizarre. He woke up one night to find himself paralysed and convinced that a probe had been shoved into his brain via his nose. He developed nosebleeds, as did his wife and son. He began to smell the odour of the aliens around his home. Symbols that the aliens had shown him appeared on his arm. He regularly suffered the sensation of missing time. He was plagued by weird memories and strange phone calls and his stereo began speaking to him. He eventually became so afraid of his flat that he moved to Connecticut, but when Connecticut proved frightening, too, he returned to New York.

Numerous psychological and physical tests were carried out, but no one could find anything wrong with Strieber. The answer, he concluded, must lie with UFOs. Hopkins had introduced him to the UFO network, but he had managed to alienate Hopkins' contacts with his eccentricities. He became paranoid about reporters, fearing that if news of his abduction experiences were made public he would be held up to ridicule, which would damage his career.

However, Strieber began to feel that he was all written out in any case: his last book had not done well and his abduction experiences were making it impossible for him to work. He therefore decided to confront his fears and to write about the abductions themselves, although he was not sure whether his experiences were real or whether they were instead memories of a former life. He nevertheless produced a manuscript for a book that he had provisionally called *Body Terror*, but one night, when his wife was asleep beside him, she spoke to him in a strange, deep voice and warned him that he should change the title to *Communion*, otherwise he would frighten people.

Strieber then circulated the manuscript. According to Hopkins, it was consistent with Strieber's horror-thriller genre rather than reading like a factual account – in one section of the manuscript, for example, the female alien led Strieber around by the penis, like a dog on a lead. Hopkins persuaded Strieber to tone it down a bit and after he had done so Strieber secured a $1,000,000 advance on the book. It was published in 1987 as *Communion: a True Story* and sold millions world-wide (Hopkins' own book, *Intruders: the Incredible Visitations at Copley Woods*, was swamped in its wake). Strieber later published four more books in the Communion series (Hopkins only managed one investigative work).

The Brooklyn Bridge abduction

After *Intruders*, Budd Hopkins' book about the Copley Wood abductions, was published Hopkins received a letter from a 41-year-old mother called Linda Napolitano. Although she did not believe in UFOs, she wrote, she had bought a copy of his book, but when she had tried to read it she had been overcome with fear and had had to put it down. She was terrified that the same cycle of abduction had been happening to her for 22 years.

When she was 19 she had been living with her parents in New York City. On one night, when she was in bed, her body had become numb and she could not move. She had had the impression that someone was in the room, but had been so frightened that she had kept her eyes tightly shut; even so, the image of a hooded figure had appeared in her mind. She knew that something terrible was happening to her and had struggled mentally against it. Sometimes she had been able to summon up the energy with which to open her lips wide enough to scream. She thought that she had screamed loudly enough to be heard a continent away – certainly her screams should have woken her parents, who sleeping in the next room, but no help had come. In the morning her parents had said that they had heard nothing and Napolitano had written it off as a bad dream. Two days later, however, the same thing had happened. She had gone to the doctor, who could find nothing wrong with her. But still these strange experiences carried on.

Five years later Napolitano got married. Although the experiences became less frequent they did not stop altogether. Even though her husband was sleeping next to her he could not hear her screams – all he could do in the morning was comfort her. Three years after her marriage Napolitano had had a baby. It was then that she had noticed a lump on the side of her nose, which made her nose crooked. She had gone to see a specialist, who had asked her why she had had surgery on her nose. She insisted that she had never had surgery on her nose, nor on any other part of her body for that matter. He replied, however, there was a scar inside her nostril that had clearly been made by a scalpel. She checked with her mother and older sister, who both confirmed that she had never had any surgery on her nose as a child.

She felt that the scar had something to do with her night-time visitations and decided to protect herself by taking the only action available to her: she stopped sleeping at night and rested during the day. The incidents did indeed cease and she also stopped talking about them, fearing that they might come back again. But her experiences still disturbed her deeply and were always something that she wanted to get to the bottom of so that she could go back to sleeping at night. After reading the opening pages of *Intruders* she therefore contacted Hopkins.

Hopkins told Napolitano that her case showed all the signs of alien abduction. Under hypnotic regression, she first recalled having seen a UFO festooned with coloured lights outside her window when she was eight, and then gradually a picture of regular UFO abductions was built up.

Then, on 30 November 1989, seven months after she had first written to Hopkins, she phoned him to tell him about an experience that she had had the night before. At around 3am, just as she was about to fall asleep, she had felt herself becoming numb. As usual, she had sensed a strange presence in the room, but this time she had kept her eyes open and had seen a small creature, with a huge head and eyes, coming at her. She then remembered floating out of the living-room window (she lived in a flat 12 stories up, two streets from FDR Drive, which runs the length of Manhattan along the East river.) Once outside, she had floated into a waiting UFO. This was the extent of her conscious memory.

Under hypnotic regression, she recalled that four or five creatures had manhandled her out of the window. They had examined her aboard the UFO and had spent some time rummaging up her nose before removing a small, metal ball. The thought had come into her mind that she did not want to have any more children. After she had been dressed and returned to her flat she had been overcome by the feeling that her children were dead – that the aliens had killed them. She had rushed into their bedroom, but could not rouse them. They were fast asleep and she had held a mirror under their noses to satisfy herself that they were still breathing.

Hopkins had taken the investigation as far as he could when he discovered that there had been witnesses to Napolitano's abduction. In February 1991 two New York policemen wrote to him to tell him that early in the morning of 30 November 1989 they had been sitting in their patrol car under an elevated section of FDR Drive when they had observed a UFO hovering above a nearby building. They had then seen a woman dressed in a nightgown, along with three ugly, little creatures, floating out of a window and into the spacecraft. Once they were all inside the UFO it had sped off towards the East river before plunging into the water near Brooklyn Bridge. It had not resurfaced.

Witnessing this incident had put them in a dilemma. It was such an outlandish tale that they did not feel that they could report it; on the other hand, they were policemen and were supposed to protect New York taxpayers like the woman concerned. For months they debated what to do about it. One of them even got to the point at which he would sit outside the building in question trying to pluck up the courage to go inside and find out whether the woman whom they had seen really existed.

Not knowing that Napolitano had already contacted him, they eventually wrote to Hopkins, asking his advice as a ufologist. It emerged that soon after the incident the policemen had indeed gone to Napolitano's flat. Even more intriguingly, there had been a third witness to the abduction: the police officers had been acting as bodyguards for a famous politician whom they had been ferrying to the New York heliport at the time. In due course Hopkins received a guarded letter from the politician concerned, who said that it was not time to tell the world about the incident. (In ufology circles the man is thought to have been the then secretary general of the United Nations, Javier Pérez de Cuéllar, although he denied it when asked directly.)

As luck would have it, another witness came forward. She had been driving over Brooklyn Bridge that night when the street lights had gone out and her car had stalled. Then she had noticed that all the cars on the bridge had come to a halt – all had had a grandstand view of the abduction of Napolitano. Sadly, she was the only one to contact Hopkins; none of the other witnesses contacted the police and the media carried no report of the abduction. Yet it was considered by some to be undoubtedly the most important alien abduction to date, and Napolitano became the darling of the UFO lobby.

The invasion of Black Brook Farm

One evening early in 1979, Joyce Bond was watching 'Coronation Street' in her family's 200-old farmhouse home, Black Brook Farm, with her three daughters – 10-year-old Susan, 12-year-old Laura and 14-year-old Jayne. At 7.30pm, just as the episode was beginning, the phone rang. It was Jayne's school friend, Sandra Streech, who lived on a farm about a quarter of a mile (40m) away. Sandra said that she and her mother had observed strange lights in the sky circling Black Brook Farm. They could hear no aircraft noise and the lights were spooky enough to set their dogs barking. (Strangely enough, the Bonds' dog remained silent.)

Joyce and the girls looked out of the window and located a large, red light hovering over the field. But Sandra had said that the lights were directly over the farmhouse, so they went outside and then saw a huge object, as big as their house, hovering over the stables. It appeared to be watching them. The UFO was covered in flashing lights and for a moment they were mesmerised, but then Joyce broke away, grabbed her daughters and they all ran back inside. They locked the doors and switched off the lights. The terrified Jayne tried to escape from the house through a small window at the back, but the others pulled her in again. Joyce phoned her husband at work and told him to come home quickly. Then the family tried to make a more organised attempt to flee – to a neighbour's house, 200 yards (183m) away – but something prevented them and they turned back.

When Mr Bond reached the village he was stopped at a police roadblock and told that there had been an accident. The sky was now full of air-

Cybermen in a scene from the TV series Dr Who and the Moonbase.

craft from the nearby airforce base, RAF Finningley, although the planes did not usually fly at night. A smallholder who lived down the road from Black Brook Farm said that he had also seen the UFO, while friends of the Bonds who lived 2 miles (3.2km) away said that they had observed a bright-red light streak upwards, into the sky, at about 9pm. Mr Bond had to take another, longer route home and as he neared the farm he saw that the top of a fence post was on fire. Subsequently, however, he found no report in the local newspaper about any accident having occurred in the village.

For years afterwards Joyce and her daughters felt that they had an incomplete memory of the event, and in 1994 they submitted to regressive hypnosis. It was a long time after their experience, however, and the hypnosis was not very successful, partly because the women were terrified of what they might recollect. But Jayne recalled having floated high above the farm, having seen bright lights and having been manhandled by a mysterious creature. The stress of the hypnotic sessions caused her hair to begin to fall out, but when the sessions were stopped it grew back.

The UFO investigators continued to keep in touch with them and all four began to report strange dreams, often involving small, grey creatures, with big, black eyes. The women told of other dreams, in which they were paralysed or naked in empty, metal rooms. The girls associated dreams of flying or being sucked up into the sky with Black Brook Farm, even though they had since grown up and moved away. Laura often dreamt of the UFO just as she was going to sleep, seeing a door open in it, but then she tended to open her eyes, being too frightened to see what happened next.

They all had the impression that Black Brook Farm was haunted. A floating, white figure had been seen nearby on several occasions, but the girls had never associated it with the UFO. When sleeping at the farm in 1990, Laura saw a glowing, white apparition approach the back door even the dog was spooked. For some reason she switched off all the lights and went upstairs in the darkness to bed. That night she felt that she had been assaulted by an alien and the next morning the dog was too frightened to go out. Jayne's husband also saw a ghost at the farm, and from 1979 it seems to have been inhabited by a poltergeist. The Bond girls' children were frightened to stay there and told of weird experiences of their own. For her part, Joyce felt a presence in the bedrooms at night; she also reported having heard laughter and sniffing, as well as anonymous assaults on the back door, and once her earring was pulled by someone whom she could not identify. Susan saw the dog levitate in 1992.

The girls also had the waking sensation of being paralysed while something in the room was holding them down and touching them; these attacks also occurred they were in their own homes, that is, not just at Black Brook Farm. Furthermore, they sometimes heard voices and saw strange lights, as well as aliens, in places other than the farm. Such encounters seemed to have been contagious: Susan's friend, Jo, for example, began to report similar experiences, while Jo's boyfriend, Martin, saw an alien while he was in Australia. The whole family lived in a constant state of fear that the Bonds' grandchildren would become affected and that the poltergeist activity would spread to their homes. The Bonds, it seems, had also been visited by 'men in black' – mysterious officials who are thought to ensure that alien abductions are kept secret by intimidating the victims.

Long-time lover

Tom's wife, Nancy, was abducted from their bedroom by alien visitors while the couple was locked in the act of sexual intercourse. They were making love when Nancy suddenly complained of an electric shock passing through her hips. Instead of thinking that he must be doing something right, Tom turned to the alarm clock and noticed that 45 minutes had passed; as far as he could remember they had only been making love for a couple of minutes.

This 'missing time' disturbed him and Tom therefore consulted a hypnotist. During a regressive-hypnosis session he recalled having seen two small aliens come into the room and then 'switch off' the couple; the two of them had frozen as if they had been hit by a tranquilliser dart. Then the aliens had lifted Tom off his wife and had carried her off. Some time later they had returned her and had placed Tom on top of her again. Fortunately, he had not lost his erection in the meantime and they had carried on where they had left off. Suddenly she had exclaimed 'Ouch', and when Tom had asked her where she felt the pain she had pointed to her hip. After that he had looked at the clock.

Nancy also consented to being regressed. Under hypnosis, she was taken back to the love-making experience and recalled a beam of blue light pointing directly at her; where it came through the window it formed a sort of entrance. It was then that she noticed that Tom was on longer on top of her, but lying beside her in a trance. Aliens were in the room. She was angry with them and told them that she wanted another baby and that by interrupting her they were messing up her fertile period. They took her away anyway. When they returned her to the bedroom they put her back in the position that she had been lying in before they appeared, with Tom lying on top of her.

12 ✦ Weird and wacky

It could be said that all alien-abduction stories are weird and wacky: for those who have no experience of abduction they certainly stretch the credulity to its limit. But some such tales are plainly from another planet.

Double trouble

At 9am on 4 January 1975 a UFO crashed into the wall of a house in São Luis, Brazil, where the teenaged Antonio Ferreira lived. The accident seems to have annoyed the aliens on board, because they later came back and zapped him with a beam of light. The aliens then emerged from the UFO and dragged Ferreira aboard. They were about 3 feet (91cm) tall, with dark hair and skin.

The aliens' chief interrogator, Croris, asked Ferreira about earthly food and cars; when the teenager's answers were not up to scratch Croris punched him in the chest. Ferreira then offered the aliens a deal: in exchange for rides to distant planets he would bring them earthly subjects for vivisection. The aliens agreed and were content to receive a cat, a dog and a parrot. In fact, they were so pleased with Ferreira that they gave him a powerful ray gun.

Ultimately, however, Ferreira found himself the subject of an experiment: he was put into a glass case along with an alien who was then miraculously transformed into his double. Ferreira then had to watch while the aliens tested whether the *doppelgänger* fooled his father.

Alien abductions are very common in Brazil, but they are not always as successful as Ferreira's. José Nobre Uchoa, a farmhand from Balem, was invited by aliens to go for a trip on the following night. He was told to walk down the middle of a motorway and that a UFO would then pick him up. Unfortunately, before the spaceship could collect Uchoa a car had flattened him.

Alien error

In 1979 the 19-year-old Franck Fontaine disappeared in France. He was happily married, with a six-month-old baby. On 26 November 1979 he had been helping his two friends, Saloman N'Diaye and Jean-Pierre Prévost, to take a van-load of clothes to the market at Gisors. Before they set off they saw a twirling lamp descending, which they took to be a UFO. N'Diaye and Prévost ran to get a camera while Fontaine drove towards the spot where the light appeared to be landing. When the two men returned they saw Fontaine's van about 200 metres (656ft) away, shrouded in light, with three equally bright lights converging on to it. The halo then rose into the sky and disappeared.

The two men ran towards the van and threw open the door, but Fontaine had gone. Even though they had no driving licences they then drove to the local police station at Cergy Pontoise, Vale D'Oise, to report Fontaine's disappearance. The police were sceptical and tested the two men for drink and drugs; subsequent interviews with their families showed that they were neither inveterate hoaxers nor practical-jokers. For a while the police believed that they had murdered Fontaine, but gruelling interrogations of the two men failed to shake their story. Detectives then circulated Fontaine's picture to other French police forces. Tests carried out on the van for radiation proved negative, while nearby air bases reported no UFO activity in that area on the day in question. The police were baffled.

Then, a week after he had disappeared, Fontaine walked into N'Diaye's flat. As far as he knew it was still 26 November. He recalled having blacked out in the light and the next thing that he knew was that he had woken up in a cabbage field near the place where he had lost consciousness. His van had gone and he assumed that it had been stolen. When they found Prévost – who was being wined and dined by a local journalist – the three men went to the police and explained the situation. By now the local constabulary was losing its patience. Convinced that the abduction was some sort of prank, the police interrogated Fontaine, but found that he could say little to enlighten them. All that he could remember was that a sphere of light the size of a tennis ball had landed on the bonnet of his van. That was all. The police were forced to release him and to close the case, unsolved.

However, due to the publicity stirred up by Prévost, the story was attracting considerable interest across France. The French science-fiction-writer Jimmy Guieu contacted the three men in the hope of writing a book about the abduction. Although Fontaine refused to undergo regressive hypnosis, Prévost volunteered to do so. And according to Prévost's recollections under hypnosis, it was he – and not Fontaine – who had been the object of the aliens' attention.

Soon after Fontaine's return Prévost said that he had been visited by a strange man called the 'travelling salesman' who had taken him to a secret, alien base in a railway tunnel on the Swiss border near the village of Bourg-de-Sirod, where Prévost had been brought up. There was a railway carriage of World War II vintage in the alien base, and people were brought there from all over the world to imbibe the wisdom of the 'intelligences from beyond', as the aliens called themselves. They sat enthralled around a campfire while an alien called Haurrio lectured them on the dangers of technology, pollution and so on.

It was later discovered that although Prévost had denied any interest in aliens and UFOs he had been reading a sci-fi story in a magazine at the time of the incident which told of a remarkably similar 'abduction'. There were also several inconsistencies in his story.

A floating bullet

The oil-field-driller Carl Hignon was a keen hunter. On 25 October 1974 he was in Medicine Bow National Forest, in Wyoming, when he saw five elks standing in a group. He raised his rifle and fired, but did not hear a report – in fact, he did not hear anything at all. Furthermore, there was no kick from the high-powered weapon and the bullet appeared to float from the barrel before falling harmlessly to the ground, 20 yards (18m) in front of him.

Hignon then turned around and saw an alien standing behind him. The creature was a humanoid, some 6 feet (1.8m) tall and weighing about 180 pounds (82kg). He had an oriental skin tone and his face seemed to blend into his neck. He wore a one-piece jump suit and his belt bore a star-shaped clasp. The alien seemed friend enough, as well as polite: 'How you doin'?' it enquired. 'Pretty good', replied Hignon. The alien then asked whether he was hungry, but before Hignon could answer a small package floated towards him. This contained four pills, which, the alien said, should last him about four days. He took one and put the other three into his pocket.

In the distance Hignon noticed a metal box. Even though it had no landing gear, no hatches and no external features of any kind he guessed that this must be the alien's ship. The alien asked him whether he wanted a ride and before Hignon could answer he found himself on board the spacecraft. It then took off and they flew to a planet that the alien said was '163,000 light miles' away. On the surface of the planet he saw buildings, including one that was tall and needle shaped; around it were lights. He put his hands over his face and complained that the lights were hurting him. 'Your sun burns us', the alien commented, somewhat inconsequentially.

The next thing that he knew was that he was stumbling down the road, still clutching his rifle. On seeing a lorry he got into it, even though he did not recognise it as his own. Using its CB radio he called for help, and when it arrived he was taken to hospital, where he kept calling for the pills that the alien had given him. Under hypnosis, Hignon filled in some of the details of his abduction. The alien's name, for example, was Ausso One.

Unusually, there was some corroborating evidence for Hignon's story.

Not only had a UFO had been reported in the area that night, but Hignon had also had the foresight to pick up the floating bullet and put it into his canteen before setting off for Ausso One's planet. Although it was badly damaged, the Carbon County Sheriff's Office identified it as coming from a 7mm Magnum rifle – the type that Hignon used. The deputy who examined it said that the bullet appeared to have been turned inside out, but could not explain how this could have happened. On the strength of this evidence alone most UFO investigators believe Hignon's story.

The Gulf Breeze abduction

Ed Walters was a UFO buff who lived in Gulf Breeze, Florida, which has long been renowned as a centre of UFO activity. Walters observed and photographed numerous alien spacecraft, but it was not until 2 December 1987 that he first saw the creatures who flew them – or so he thought.

He awoke during the Wednesday night in question to hear a baby cry. This was strange because he and his wife, Frances, did not have a baby at that time, neither were there any babies in his house nor, as far as he knew, were there any in his neighbours' houses. Then he heard voices discussing the crying baby in Spanish. Walters grabbed his pistol and, along with his wife, checked the house for Cubans. When they were sure that the house was free of illegal immigrants they went out of the French windows into the back garden to see a UFO swooping down from the skies and halt about 100 feet (30.5m) above the pool. Walters and his wife ran back into the house; as they cowered inside Walters heard a voice commanding him to 'step forward'.

A veteran ufologist, Walters grabbed his Polaroid camera before he stepped out with his gun. When he reached the pool he pulled out the camera and took a photograph. The flash went off and suddenly he felt terribly exposed, so he fled back into the house and locked the French windows. Peeping through the kitchen window, Walters and his wife watched as the UFO sped off into the distance. During the encounter, Walters had felt a strange buzzing in his head, but now it faded.

Walters and his wife returned to bed, but then the dog barked – just once. This was unusual, so Walters again grabbed his gun and camera and went downstairs to the French windows. An experienced UFO-watcher, he was certain that he would see the alien spacecraft. But when he pulled back the curtain he was instead confronted by something beyond his wildest imaginings: just inches in front of him was a humanoid. Although it was about 4 feet (1.2m) tall, with big, black eyes, it was not like the greys that most other people see: this one was wearing a helmet with a transparent visor pulled down over its eyes (this apparently enabled it to see on Earth).

Walters, usually a pillar of steel when it came to snapping UFOs, was so taken aback that he forgot to photograph the alien. He screamed, backed away, tripped and fell backwards, still brandishing the gun. He was determined to shoot the alien if it tried to get into the house. The creature seemed to get the message, for when Walters picked himself up he could see it retreating. It was still only 20 feet (6m) away, however, and certain that he could capture it he put down both the camera and gun in order to unlock the French windows. But a trap had been set: as soon as Walters set foot outside a beam of blue light struck him and seemed to nail his feet to the floor. Then he was lifted up by his legs, causing Walters to reach for the door and his wife to grab him and pull him free. Demonstrating admirable self-possession, Walters seized the camera and took a photograph of the UFO, which was hovering 50 feet (15m) above the patio, but he again failed to take a picture of the alien. The alien spacecraft then sent out another blue beam, which Walters believed picked up the alien that he had seen and beamed it aboard.

As a UFO enthusiast, Walters naturally consented to undergo regressive hypnosis. Once in a hypnotic trance he revealed that he had undergone a series of abductions. Locked away among his repressed memories was the recollection of an encounter that had happened when he was 17 years old. He remembered having been followed by a big, black dog when he was cycling to a shop. The dog had waited for him and had then followed him home – no matter how fast he had cycled it had still kept up with him. That night he had been tormented by the thought that there was something in the house and that it might jump on to the bed. The dog, apparently, was an alien.

There seems to have been a deep memory block regarding what happened next, because Walters then fast-forwarded to 1 May 1988, four-and-a-half months after he had seen the alien through the French windows. This time he remembered that he had been abducted. A rod had been forced up his nose and he recalled lying on the floor covered with a sticky residue. There were four aliens with him; three wore protective shields, while the other was dressed in a tight, pink body suit. They were all carrying silver sticks.

Like many other abductees, he had then found himself in a large room which had a table in it. Underneath the table he spotted what he thought was a serial number. (He later reproduced the symbols that he noted, but they were not publicly released because they were being kept secret by senior UFO investigators to check the veracity of future sightings, Walters said.) While Walters was under the table, another creature, which had white hair, entered the room. Walters was then zapped by blue beam, which instantly transported him onto the table. After that a gang of aliens came in; their skin-tight body suits matched the colour of their skins so perfectly that they might as well have been nude. They carried a smaller creature – maybe only 2 feet (60cm) tall – with them, who was darker grey in colour. The aliens seem to have probed Walter's mind, stirring up all sorts of unwanted memories.

As the hypnotic sessions continued Walters revealed memories of a series of long-forgotten abductions which had begun when he was a teenager. They all involved creatures with strange, long-fingered hands, which resembled the alien hands described by Leonard Stringfield. (Unfortunately, Stringfield later revealed that these hands were part of a hoax – a hoax, in fact, that long predated alien abductions: a showman had once displayed them, claiming that they were the hands of a mermaid.)

Abducted in the bath

British abductions are often more prosaic. In February 1976, for example, in Keighley, West Yorkshire, two tall aliens, with cat-like eyes and grey faces, appeared in the bedroom of an ambulance-driver named Reg. Although they observed him as though he were some sort of specimen, they seemed to need his talents. He was a dab hand at fixing things and the aliens showed him a piece of rubber tubing and asked him to come with them.

They told him to lie on the bed and then they paralysed him. Soon he found himself floating through the ceiling and up to a waiting UFO, which Reg said looked like a bathtub. In common with other abductees, once inside the UFO he was laid on a bed and given a full medical examination. A large, purple device, which looked like an eye, was scanned across his body. The aliens who had abducted Reg kept quoting the Bible at him, but when he asked them who they were they replied rather rudely 'An insignificant being such as a worm should not ask such questions'. However, they did volunteer that 'a thousand of your years are but a day to us'.

Suddenly Reg found himself back in his bed; he was still paralysed, but

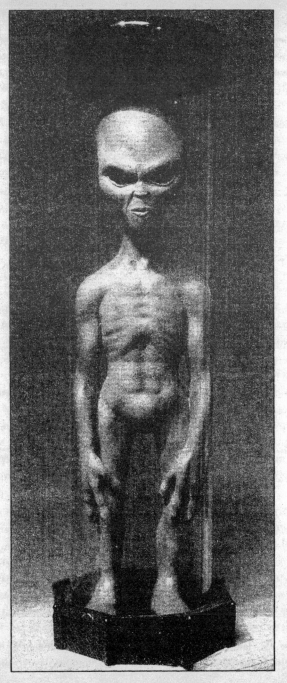

Detailed mode
an alien, show
the large fore
and big, dark
as described
times by
abductees.

the feeling of numbness soon wore off. Although there were large chunks of recollection missing from his memory he nevertheless immediately contacted the British Unidentified Flying Object Research Association and told it his story.

A Persian-carpet ride

During the late 1970s Dr Simon Taylor lived and worked in Tehran as an instructor for the Iranian Air Force. On 16 September 1976 he went with an Iranian friend named Reza to the village of Ahar, in the Elburz mountains to the north of the city. They arrived at around 6pm and stayed in a mountainside cabin near the shrine. After dinner they went to bed early, but then Taylor awoke, gasping for breath, in the middle of the night. He saw Reza fiddling with the paraffin lamp, thinking that it must be faulty, when the cabin was rocked by a loud pounding. Fearing that it was about to collapse around them, Taylor and Reza ran outside.

Then, in the darkness, they saw three men dressed in black; they had large, Mongoloid eyes. Taylor feared that members of the shah's notorious secret police had come to arrest Reza, but that thought passed from his mind when they started communicating with him and Reza telepathically. They were told not to be afraid and were given time to dress before their abductors marched them down a mountain path. After a while they felt lush, Persian rugs beneath their feet. Before they knew it they were in round room and were being invited to sit cross-legged on the carpeted floor and to look out of a huge window that seemed to take up the whole of one wall. They could see the distant lights of the city through it.

The room began to shake before shooting upwards, into the air; Taylor could feel the pressure building up in his eardrums. He could see Tehran beneath them, and then other great cities of the world – along with his native Birmingham. They were also privileged to enjoy the sight of aerial panoramas of some of the planet's greatest landscapes, such as mountain ranges, deserts and icecaps. The creatures gave them a telepathic commentary on this whistle-stop, guided tour of the world and also revealed that they lived on Earth, but in places in which humans hardly ever encountered them. Suddenly it was all over and Taylor and Reza found themselves back on the ground, not far from the place from which they had been abducted. It was 2pm.

Three days later there was a particularly detailed UFO sighting in the area. Lights were seen in the sky and two F4 Phantom jets were scrambled from Shahrokhi Air Force Base. The first suffered electrical failure as it approached the UFO, but when it turned away its equipment started working again. The second locked its radar on to the UFO and ascertained that the object was the size of a Boeing 707. The pilot thought that he saw the UFO launching a missile, but when he tried to respond with a missile of his own the plane's electrical system failed; as with the first jet, however, when he turned away everything returned to full working order.

Even more spookily, immediately after the abduction Reza told Taylor that he knew when and how he would die; he also revealed these details to his family. In early 1987 Reza was hospitalised with cancer of the liver. A few days before he died he checked out of the hospital and went to a shrine dedicated to Imam Reza, a descendant of Mohammed, where he handed out money. The next morning he was found dead in the room in which he was staying. There were no indications of suicide or foul play.

Military abductions

Some have suggested that UFO witnesses have been abducted by military personnel in an effort to keep a lid on the UFO question, the reasoning being that if the public knew of the real extent of alien visits to this world then there would be widespread panic and civil disorder. Dr Helmut Lammer, of the Austrian Space Research Institute, has studied the subject, which, in ufology circles, is called military abductions of UFO witnesses (MILABs).

In his preliminary report on MILABs, which was published in 1996, Lammer found that the unmarked helicopters that are used for these abductions have been photographed on several occasions. There are usually other unmarked vehicles around when the victims are snatched, too. Military abductees are typically disorientated at the outset, either by drugs or a powerful, electromagnetic field. Then they are taken by helicopter or van to an underground facility, where they are subjected to medical examinations similar to those carried out by aliens. (However, one way in which to tell whether you have been snatched by the military or by aliens is by looking at the shape of the room: aliens examine their abductees in circular rooms, the military uses square ones.) Microchips are then implanted into abductees by means of a syringe; they are usually placed behind the ear and may transmit psychological data to a central data bank. (Interestingly, some abductees, such as Christa Tilton, say that they have seen aliens working alongside humans in underground facilities.)

According to Dr Lammer, 'MILABs may be evidence that a secret military/intelligence task force has been in operation in North America since the early 1980s, and is involved in the monitoring and kidnapping of alleged UFO abductees'. The purpose of such abductions seems to be to take out any alien implants and insert implants of their own, as well as to examine women to see if they have been impregnated with hybrid foetuses.

An alien partnership

The 28-year-old Mynra Hansen and her six-year-old son were driving near the town of Cimmarron, New Mexico, when they saw five flying saucers land and capture a cow. The aliens mutilated the cow and then abducted the mother and son. The humans were informed telepathically that the cruel mutilation of a live beast was necessary.

Inside the spacecraft, Hansen was forced to strip. The aliens, who were hairless, were particularly amused by her bodily hair, especially her eyebrows and eyelashes. A vaginal probe was inserted, which gave her an unpleasant infection that persisted for some time afterwards. The aliens, she said, shuffled instead of walked. Their ribs poked out and they looked unwell. A strange-looking being then appeared; he was naked from the waist up, and, like the other aliens, was thin and scrawny. He apologised to Hansen, saying that her abduction had been a mistake; her son was alright and his crewmen would be punished. Throughout the trip Hansen had the impression that the aliens did not seem to know what they were doing, which she found far from reassuring.

On looking out of the window Hansen saw a planet – not the Earth – and stars beyond it. She was later escorted outside the craft by some other aliens, who were better dressed, and recognised the landscape to be that around Roswell, New Mexico. She was also taken down by elevator to a huge, underground facility, which seemed to be manned by grey aliens and human beings in equal numbers. Glimpsing her son, she gave her guide the slip and set off after the boy. She soon became lost, however, and found herself in a dimly lit room that contained large tanks that were full of fluid and floating human body parts. It was then that her alien guides caught up with her; they found her squatting in a corner of the room, crying.

After that she was reunited with her son. They were subjected to blinding flashes of light, which, she understood, were supposed to erase all memory of what they had seen. Then they and their car were flown back to the place from which they had been abducted before being released. They drove home having retained no memory of the abduction (her account was later related under hypnosis). Hansen maintained that scans had subsequently revealed the presence of implants in her brain, which, she said, had been inserted by the aliens during her abduction.

Only half abducted

In May 1973 Judy Doraty was driving with four other members of her family near Houston, Texas, when all five of them saw a bright light in the sky which appeared to be following them. Doraty recalled pulling over and getting out of the car in order to take a better look, but could not remember what had happened next.

This memory lapse annoyed her so much that seven years later she underwent regressive hypnosis. It was then she recalled that she had had what ufologists call a 'bi-locational experience' (in which the victim seems to be in two places at once): Doraty had simultaneously been standing by her car and aboard the alien craft. The aliens had used a strange beam of yellow light, which had particles swirling within it, with which to capture a calf, which they cruelly mutilated. They then apparently used various parts of its body to check the spread of a dangerous toxin.

The aliens appeared to be conventional greys – short and thin, with large heads, pale skins and tiny noses and mouths – but although they had large eyes they were not the black, featureless orbs that other greys have: this race had vertical, cat-like pupils and yellow irises. The aliens apologised to Doraty, explaining that she had been brought on board – or half brought on board – by mistake. Yet she caught a glimpse of her daughter being operated on by the aliens in the spacecraft. They assured her, however, that they did not intend to harm either of them.

Getting our own back

The question remains: if aliens are always abducting humans, have humans ever abducted aliens? The answer is: they just might have. The aliens who were supposed to have been captured in the so-called 'Roswell Incident' were all dead, so this cannot really be called an abduction. However, there was an incident in the city of Varginha, Brazil, in 1996 that might just fit the bill. Varginha is a city of 150,000 souls, situated north-east of São Paulo and around 160 miles (257km) from the coast. During the mid-1990s there were numerous UFO sightings in the area.

On 20 January 1996 Varginha's Fire Department received a number of calls from people reporting a strange creature that was abroad in the area. Four men were accordingly sent to apprehend it and when they arrived at the site of one sighting a crowd of people directed them to some woods. They were told that they had better hurry, as children were throwing rocks at the creature, so the firemen rushed down the hill towards the woods. There they saw what ufologists call a classic grey. It was short, with long, spindly arms, a big head, large eyes and no genitals; it also wore no clothes. But the odd thing about this grey was that it was red and shiny, as if it had been rubbed with baby oil; it furthermore smelt of ammonia. The creature put up no resistance and, with the help of net, the firemen caught it easily. It appeared to be angry, however, because it made a buzzing noise like a swarm of hornets. They dragged it up the hill, put it in a covered box and loaded it on to a lorry. Then they called the army, which took it away; military vehicles were later seen in the area.

About six hours later, three local girls – the 22-year-old Andrade Xavier, the 16-year-old Liliane Fatima and the 14-year-old Valquira Fatima – were taking a short cut home from work when they bumped into another strange creature. This one had three lumps on its head and big, red eyes and it was standing with one hand between its legs. They thought that it was the devil and ran home screaming. When the Fatima girls got home they told their mother what they had seen. She went back to the spot, but the creature had gone. However, there was a strong smell of ammonia in the air and some strange footprints could be seen in the mud.

Two days later a dead creature answering this general description was seen in a box that was being loaded on to a military vehicle. The story soon spread that seven aliens in all had been captured, including the dead one; two of them were badly injured. It was also said that five more were in the area and had gone into hiding. There were reports that creatures had been taken to hospital for medical treatment, as well as to the University of Campinas, where they would be studied. There were furthermore rumours that two USAF officers had been seen entering a local hospital, presumably to inspect the aliens. Two aliens – one male, one female – were said to have been taken from the hospital to the University of São Paulo under the escort of the USAF officers.

A young man who claimed to be a relative of a Brazilian soldier tried to sell a film purporting to show a captive alien to a Brazilian TV network for a mere $68,000, but his offer was turned down. However, UFO investigators say that they have spoken to people who say that they have seen the footage.

By this time alien fever had reached such a pitch of excitement that a city official suggested changing the name of a local park to Seite Extreterrestes – the 'Seven Extraterrestrials'. The US *Wall Street Journal* then picked up on the story; although all the officials to whom the paper's journalists spoke denied any knowledge of the captured aliens the army could not explain what its lorries had been doing in Varginha at the time in question. By then 60 witnesses had claimed to have seen a cigar-shaped UFO crash in the area. Furthermore, videotaped interviews of men in civilian dress who claimed to be part of the army detail which had rounded up the aliens were in circulation, although the paper said that it was impossible to determine the tapes' authenticity. Some of the original witnesses were now demanding $200 an interview, while a documentary about the incident that was aired on Brazilian television was so popular that it was repeated the following weekend.

But then Brazil – even more so than the USA – has long been home to UFO sightings, as well as to doctored photographs and other palpable UFO hoaxes. (Not that one would wish to dent the veracity of Antônio Villas-Boas' story – there are too many men out there, hoping.)